Auditing Business Continuity Management Plans

Assess and Improve Your Performance Against ISO 22301

Second Edition

John Silltow

First published in the UK in 2008
by

BSI
389 Chiswick High Road
London W4 4AL

Second edition published in 2012
© British Standards Institution 2012

Typeset in Sabon by Monolith – http://www.monolith.uk.com
Printed in Great Britain by Berforts Group, www.berforts.co.uk

British Library Cataloguing in Publication Data
A catalogue record for this book is available from the British Library

ISBN 978-0-580-74342-9

Contents

Introduction

The purpose of this book is simple: it is to help make organizations better prepared for incidents and their recovery. How it goes about this is a little more complex.

Most managers will be familiar with the concept of internal audit. Its role is to assess and evaluate the activities and functions of an organization against standards, guidelines, best practice and regulatory issues, to form a view on whether those activities or functions are performing effectively. Audit can then provide recommendations or views on how functions and processes may be changed to improve efficiency or reduce risks. Using the results of these audit reviews from across the organization the head of audit can then provide an assurance statement to top management.

This role uniquely places internal auditors in the situation of having to understand systems and processes at a sufficient depth to make recommendations on their improvement as well as being conscious of the risks that both drive an organization or function forward as well as threatening its very existence. Their views have to be balanced with operational needs in formulating their assurance statements.

This book is therefore written with the internal auditor as the core focus. It achieves its aims by providing the depth of information and knowledge that is needed to understand each part of the business continuity process. It also looks at the risks and threats that exist.

There are other players within and external to an organization that will have a direct or review role within the business continuity project and programmes. Few of them will work to the same depth as internal audit and all of them will find some value in this book, perhaps from a better understanding of an issue or a greater appreciation of how one thing impacts another.

Internal audit is not an operational function responsible for making decisions but rather it is charged with evaluating operational decisions in relation to the achievement of organizational objectives. When it comes to a project as large and complex as business continuity there is a good case for audit being a part of the project team, albeit in an advisory role. It still remains for the business and the appropriate managers to make the decisions, but by using their audit team as advisers they will have on board experts in risk and control who will input information and ideas that may not have been considered before.

Whilst the book has been built around experience and research, it also draws on the International Standard ISO 22300 family. This set of Standards generically entitled *Societal security* form a comprehensive basis on which to build a business continuity management system. These Standards have been developed from the British Standard BS 25999, *Business continuity management* and other related Standards as well as contributions from many people and organizations around the world. Certification to ISO 22301:2012 *Societal security — Business continuity management systems — Requirements* can be achieved by any organization.

Every section of the book provides an audit view with suggestions for some of the subject areas that can be reviewed. Some of these are supplemented by 'audit scope' ideas to help frame a potential audit and get the best out of any reviews. Many suggestions cover issues that the business continuity project team will also look at. This is not to imply that work should be unnecessarily re-performed, merely that where aspects are important auditors should be sure that the work has been, or will be, completed. In some cases who actually achieves the piece of work will not be particularly important.

Examples from real life are used to highlight some of the issues. Mostly these are not the headline-grabbing incidents but those where staff were out of their depth or unhappy or where nobody thought ahead to the consequences of a particular decision. They all illustrate how easy it is to 'just miss' and end up either poorly prepared or with an incident.

Inevitably there is overlap in the book between chapters. Business continuity is a relatively simple concept but the ramifications are complex. This means that the same items come up from different perspectives as the story evolves. The overlap should, however, reinforce the message and allow for different perceptions to be explored. It also allows for the reader to dip into chapters without reading the book right through. This can be very useful if you have a simple audit to do and just need some quick ideas.

1

Overview of business continuity and the role of audit

Setting the scene

This chapter provides an overview of business continuity planning and looks at the role of audit within the business continuity management framework. It considers the different types of audit and their place in the process. From this it highlights that the internal auditor conducts the most detailed review work and therefore has most input to a business continuity programme.

Introduction

Business continuity management is not about creating a great plan that, once written, sits in a desk drawer and gathers dust. It is not about creating a great plan and not telling anyone about it. It's not about letting consultants build a great plan for you and then expecting all staff to welcome it with open arms and immediately adopt it.

It is about working with staff, unions, emergency services, partners, suppliers and many others to build a plan that all can work with and all can see the sense in. It's about involving the emergency services who just may have to rescue your staff. It's about communicating with your staff who may, one morning, find their place of work is no longer accessible due to flooding. It's about reassuring your customers who have paid you to provide a service and you cannot because your factory has no power. It's about satisfying your neighbours and the public at large that while your business is burning down you are minimizing the impact upon them. It's about telling people what is going on in a full and positive manner.

Essentially business continuity management involves:

- identifying the organization's key products and services;
- identifying the prioritized activities and resources required to deliver them;
- evaluating the threats to these activities and their dependencies;
- putting arrangements in place to resume these activities following an incident;
- making sure that these arrangements will be effective in all circumstances.

This is not a small exercise and should not be considered a quick task.

Overview of business continuity

Business continuity management can be defined as the management process that provides a framework for building capability that safeguards the objectives of the organization including its obligations.

Essentially therefore business continuity planning continually confronts the likelihood or otherwise of an incident. Such a business interruption may be something minor or major, but the important thing is that there are processes in place to enable management control to be gained when it does occur.

Depending on the length or severity of the interruption, significant consequences or the very sustainability of the organization may hinge on management's ability to re-establish critical business functions. Usually these business functions have been established and developed over a period of years, but management must rebuild and get them up and running within hours or days of the business interruption. This is a difficult situation and rebuilding the complex business environment in a timely manner requires a well thought-out plan in place ready to be executed.

Business continuity planning is therefore the main answer to an unexpected business interruption. It is a proactive management-led incident management programme driven by business requirements.

There is, however, one other aspect that should not be overlooked. The very act of reviewing the business and its processes will identify areas that need to be strengthened or altered to enable them to cope. By its very nature, therefore, an exercise to build business continuity in an organization will strengthen that organization against incidents.

Consider the not-for-profit organization with three separate buildings. When it decided to implement a business continuity system, its review of

IT systems identified that all IT traffic was routed through building 1. This meant it had both a traffic bottleneck and a single point of failure. These issues automatically increased its chances of an incident. Consequently it introduced a new connection between buildings 2 and 3 that meant that voice and data traffic could then be routed directly between buildings or re-routed if there was a problem. As a result it increased its resilience before it even developed any business continuity plans.

No organization can have complete control over the business environment in which it operates. There are a number of issues that will be outside its control, from the weather, through the utility services to the attitudes of staff and customers.

There are external influences, such as regulations and industry guidelines, that support the promotion of greater resilience among organizations, public agencies and the wider local community.

There are also the standard external threats for all organizations, such as fire, flood, power outages, epidemics and terrorism. These do not discriminate between the not-for-profit, private or public sector, or between large, medium and small organizations. However, all those sectors and businesses have their own threats and risks in addition, which need to be faced as part of the price of doing business.

Consequently, every organization needs to have in place a plan to recover key business processes following an incident. The recovery plan, however, has to consider not just likely events, but also those that may be considered unlikely or perhaps even impossible.

A process like scenario planning that formulates strategies for organizations that are way beyond that organization's everyday business assumptions may be useful to outline some of these 'unthinkable' options. With this process the business works through the key 'what if' scenarios that face it to develop solutions. Most of these will be the normal extensions to business risk, such as a key supplier collapsing or a new rival product, but some will be pitched well beyond this. Considerations such as currency devaluation, finite supplies of a key commodity running out and sequestration of assets may be part of these 'what if' scenarios.

Just as the organization can develop strategies to deal with all these 'what if' options, it can also build some or all of these into its business continuity management processes to ensure it can survive if the worst happens.

Some of these 'what if' options are global in nature and there are recommendations that all businesses include such threats in their business continuity plans. An example of this is the risk of a bird-flu pandemic. Much has been published on this subject to help all businesses understand this risk and take steps to ensure that there is a continuity plan in place to prevent it from destroying the business.

The other point about a business continuity process is that it needs to match the organization. It may sound obvious, but a large organization needs a large plan while a small organization needs a small one. This aspect clearly has an impact on the cost and time involved in building a plan and in the recovery processes put in place.

While dealing with the incidents that are likely to affect an organization, the plan must be realistic and achievable. Failure to do this will lead to the plan falling into disuse and being unusable if the time comes to rely on it.

The plan creates an incident management team empowered by top managment or equivalent to control any interruptions of the business. Properly constructed, this incident management team has the capability of responding appropriately to any interruption of any scale. If the incident is then found to be one that was envisaged and planned for, the appropriate business continuity plan can be invoked.

As a management controlled programme, a business continuity plan reduces, by a variety of means, the consequences of a business interruption to a level acceptable to management. Because of the processes involved in building the plan, it also provides a tested approach that, when invoked, will enable a known and agreed level of recovery to take place.

This can be achieved because each business function has been analysed to define the consequences of an outage of service. These consequences are then assessed by management, which defines the point at which the consequences are unacceptable. That point becomes the recovery time frame, although it is also known as the recovery time objective. Each business function may have a separate recovery time objective.

The business continuity plan identifies the recovery alternatives that cost-effectively restore critical business functions within an acceptable time frame. In doing this it needs to take into account the time that the business process can remain functioning in a limited way. This duration is known as the maximum tolerable period of disruption. At the end of that period the business function will no longer be recoverable.

Management authorizes and approves the recovery solutions. As a result, the recovery plan is developed around the recovery solution authorized by management.

The business continuity plan objectives are to:

- ensure continuity and survival of the business;
- provide protection of corporate assets;
- provide management control of risks and exposures;
- provide preventative measures where appropriate;
- take proactive management control of any business interruption.

Business continuity planning provides a balance between acceptable potential losses and acceptable one-time and annual costs. The business continuity plan can also assist management in providing customer confidence and service satisfaction, as incident management control can assist the business in maintaining market share, and can provide the basis to promote a positive image.

Subsequent chapters will deal with all these issues in greater detail but as a pictorial overview to the processes involved, Figure 1 may prove helpful.

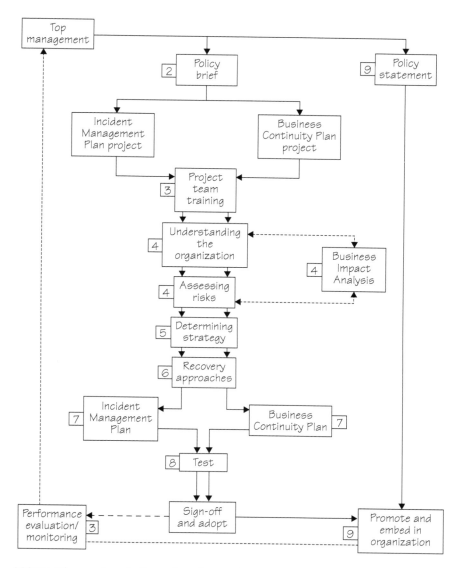

NOTE: The numbers indicate the relevant chapters

Figure 1 Business continuity process flow diagram

The role of audit

Organizations are structured to have several lines of defence, although they may not generally consider it that way. These are shown in Figure 2 below.

Essentially, the first line is the operational managers and staff who have the day-to-day responsibility for managing the organization's risks. The risk management functions look after the second line with internal audit providing an independent assessment of work of the first two lines.

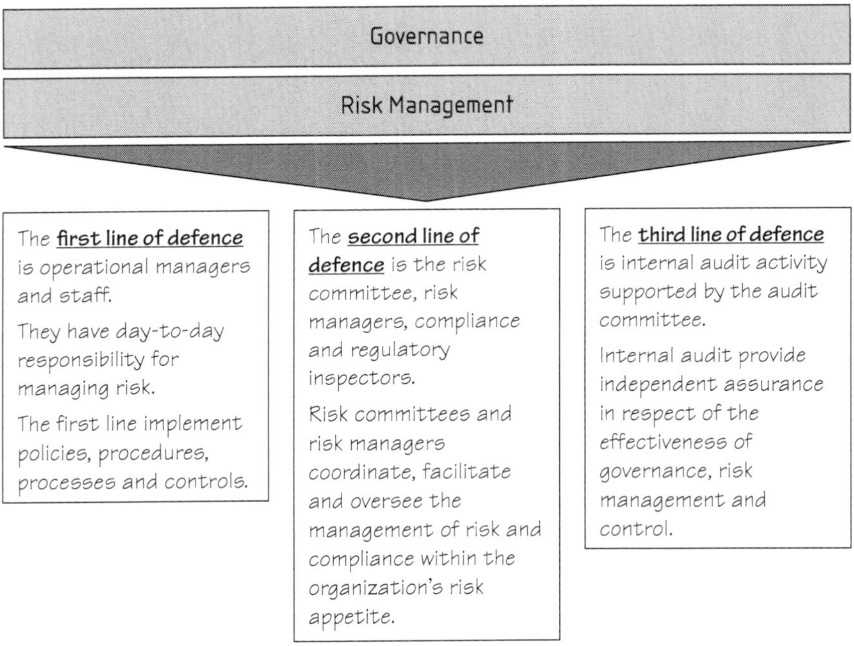

Governance
Risk Management

The **first line of defence** is operational managers and staff.	The **second line of defence** is the risk committee, risk managers, compliance and regulatory inspectors.	The **third line of defence** is internal audit activity supported by the audit committee.
They have day-to-day responsibility for managing risk.		Internal audit provide independent assurance in respect of the effectiveness of governance, risk management and control.
The first line implement policies, procedures, processes and controls.	Risk committees and risk managers coordinate, facilitate and oversee the management of risk and compliance within the organization's risk appetite.	

Figure 2 The three lines of defence

The definition of 'audit' contained in ISO 22301, is:

'Systematic, independent and documental process for obtaining audit evidence and evaluating it objectively to determine the extent to which the audit criteria are fulfilled.'

There are two main categories of audit that most organizations will be familiar with:

Internal audit

Internal audit is an independent, objective assurance and consulting activity designed to add value and improve an organization's operations. It provides assurance that the risks the organization is exposed to are being effectively managed. These risks include those relating to business continuity management. The role, responsibilities and accountability of internal audit is defined in its charter, which is approved by the audit committee and senior management.

Larger organizations may also have other functions such as compliance, operational risk, quality and health and safety, which also contribute to the assurance process.

External audit

External audit is a statutory function charged with ensuring the accuracy and veracity of the annual report and accounts. To achieve this, the external auditors will undertake their own assurance work, which can include an assessment of business continuity plans. They will also place reliance to a greater or lesser degree on the work conducted by the internal audit function, if there is one.

Other review bodies

Whilst there are a number of potential review bodies, for business continuity purposes there are some others that need specifically to be considered.

Compliance

Compliance auditing is the second line of defence. It has the role of examining and evaluating defined activities of an organization to measure adherence to legal, regulatory, contractual and procedural obligations. Essentially compliance auditing determines whether a process or transaction has or has not followed applicable rules. If rules are not complied with, the auditor determines the cause and recommends ways to prevent future non-compliances.

The rules being tested can be:

- those created by the organization for itself through its policies, plans and procedures;
- those imposed on the organization through external laws and regulations; or
- those external standards that the organization has chosen to follow (e.g. ISO 22301).

Many organizations have a specific compliance function. That function may have its own independent reporting line or it may become a part of internal audit but separate to the day-to-day work. Sitting within audit can make compliance functions more powerful as they can then also report through the audit committee.

Certification audit

Organizations wishing to obtain certification to ISO 22301 will need to undergo audits by an external assessor (or certification body) approved by their country's accreditation body. These accreditation bodies are members of the International Accreditation Forum (IAF), which has established Multilateral Recognition Arrangements (MLA) between its accreditation body members. These reduce risk to business and its customers by ensuring that an accredited certificate may be relied upon anywhere in the world.

The compliance audits by the certification body take place at specific stages of the project and then regularly after the certification is awarded (Appendix 1). In performing these compliance audits the certification body can rely on the work undertaken by other auditors, including internal, external and compliance auditors.

Essentially a certification audit is similar to a compliance audit. The difference is that the auditors are acting on behalf of the standards body and have been accredited to undertake this specific task.

Organization

ISO 22301 puts a strong focus on the organization having control systems in place to monitor, measure and analyse performance and thus to be able to address adverse trends or results. Such nonconformities need to be identified and then suitable action taken to control, contain or correct them, along with any consequences arising.

Suitable documentation needs to be developed to enable issues and findings to be recorded as well as logging any actions taken. Such documentation needs to be retained and protected against any future need.

The Standard also expects top management to review the business continuity management system (BCMS) at planned intervals to ensure its continuing suitability, adequacy and effectiveness. These reviews should take into account follow-up actions from previous reviews as well as the need for any change or opportunity for improvement.

In addition, the organization may choose to have a dedicated team to undertake self-assessment audits and/or to employ external consultants for all or part of the project. Depending upon the contract, the external consultants may then be responsible for all detailed review and audit work or they in turn may work with others, such as internal audit and other business functions.

Focus on internal audit

Internal audit, unlike any other review body noted, has a remit to provide assurance to management. For this reason, internal audit will have to undertake a greater depth of review to be able to fully understand how the various processes and activities operate and interact. It cannot provide any valid assurance until it has done so. The primary focus of this book, therefore, is on the role of the internal audit function. However, certification auditors, compliance auditors, external auditors, consultants and others in the business continuity sphere will also find this material very useful.

That internal audit is expected to undertake detailed audit reviews does not prevent others from undertaking the same or similar work. However, directing this book at this more detailed level provides a wider scope for ensuring that the business continuity process is appropriate, robust and fit for purpose.

Providing assurance

There are three primary roles for internal audit within business continuity:

- to provide independent and objective assurance to management on the business continuity management framework;
- to contribute as consultants to the business continuity process if required;
- to take part in the organizational approach to contingency planning and consider the risks to its own activities.

The primary purpose of providing assurance to management is a simple concept that is identified in the audit charter and underpinned by a wide variety of activities designed to ensure that when audit provides assurance to management it knows:

- what aspects are encompassed in the business it is reporting on;
- that the process conforms (as far as possible) to best practice in the sector or marketplace;
- that risks taken are commensurate with the risk appetite of the business; and
- that mitigating strategies, offsetting activities and/or residual risks are known and recorded.

Assurance mapping

While top management is responsible for ensuring that business-critical risks are being assured and adequately managed, the task of assurance is often provided by a broad range of functions.

For example, assurance can be provided from a number of sources both internal and external and can provide confidence to stakeholders, comfort to managers and trust and credibility to the organization. However, ineffective or over assurance can become burdensome, impacting on the effectiveness of front line service delivery.

Increasingly, therefore, 'assurance maps' are being requested by audit committees who want to take comfort in the knowledge that all of the pieces of the assurance jigsaw are joined up, with no gaps in coverage and the minimum of assurance overlaps.

An assurance map is therefore a tool to ensure key risks are assured across the organization.

The assurance mapping process is concerned with identifying all of the sources of assurance received across the organization. Once identified, the information can then be collated and analysed in order to provide a better understanding of the roles and scope of the work undertaken by the various assurance providers both within and external to the organization.

The primary drivers for the assurance mapping process are:

- To inform internal audit planning – through the identification of assurance provided from other review and inspection bodies, to avoid duplication and identify potential assurance gaps to key risk areas.
- To inform the annual governance statement – this requires an indication of the level of assurance that the systems and processes that comprise the organization's governance arrangements can provide.
- To ensure sources of assurance are properly reported and that appropriate action is being taken on risk and internal control related issues identified by the internal and external auditors and other review and inspection bodies.

Auditors as consultants

Because internal audit is part of the business and is aware of the day-to-day constraints and issues, as well as the risks and risk appetite of the business, it is well placed to be part of any business continuity programme.

The role of internal audit, however, is advisory and as such it cannot make operational decisions, as this would conflict with its independence. For example if an auditor made the decision that a business would use a specific supplier for stationery purchases, then the audit department would have lost its independence on the matter and could not subsequently review that decision.

It is recognized within the audit profession that while there is an absolute requirement for independence, there may also be a wealth of skills within the audit department that management could use to its advantage in undertaking fairly specific operational tasks. In view of this it is possible for an auditor to be engaged by management as a 'consultant' to undertake one or more tasks. The difference here is that the consultancy is covered by a contract drawn up by management, and that the auditor is acting in his or her own capacity. Any operational decisions they make are under that contract and this does not prevent another auditor from subsequently reviewing those decisions and having the independence to make a judgement on them.

Business continuity for the audit function

The business continuity plan for internal audit, as for most other support functions, should be based upon developing a controlled resumption of the service as space and equipment becomes available and as the business returns to full operation.

In the short term, during a recovery, it may be appropriate to release internal audit staff to the business to assist in operational activities or to carry out special reviews to ensure that any revised procedures introduced during the emergency still provide an adequate degree of operational control.

Risk

Within business continuity there is frequent mention of 'risk'. It is therefore worth considering this aspect a little further here. A fuller overview of risk and some of the tools for assessing it are discussed in Appendix 2.

Although risk appears in business continuity terms as a threat to an organization or system, it can also be a positive. Identifying a risk (or weakness) may provide the organization with the opportunity to change the system, or process, involved and turn the risk to an advantage (an opportunity). So undertaking the investigations and analyses required to determine a business continuity system may lead to changes in organizational behaviour to the advantage of the organization, its staff and systems.

A risk assessment is required to identify key sources of risk within an organization, reduce them where possible and ultimately provide the basis for the development of containment and/or recovery measures. In order to achieve this, it is important to understand the likelihood of a particular threat occurring, identify its causes and evaluate the potential effects on the business.

Of course, these factors can change markedly between risks, organizations and sectors. For example a communications failure could cause serious losses in a matter of minutes within a financial institution but may not impact a manufacturing process for some hours. Conversely a delivery delay could wreak havoc in a 'just in time' manufacturing environment while only mildly affecting a financial institution.

All organizations therefore need to be aware of the risks that they face in everyday trading. These will include:

- business risks – e.g. a competing business;
- data risks – e.g. loss or compromise of data;
- environmental risks – e.g. weather-related activities like floods;
- regulatory risks – e.g. new legislation that affects business trading;
- personnel risks – e.g. low morale among staff leading to poor customer service;
- reputational risk – e.g. product recalls that lead to loss of confidence in a brand.

There are many types of risks and it must be emphasized that the above list is just a small selection of high-level ones.

Risk is therefore the awareness that something threatens the organization. The next stage is to consider how this risk could materialize. The above list provides an example in each selected category but there are many others. One that should never be overlooked is the risk that your surrounding businesses and neighbours bring.

Consider the following real examples.

- *The head office of a financial institution was located very close to an army reserve base. Any bomb threat or other incident at the army facility closed the road leading to the financial institution.*
- *In another location a bomb had actually exploded. The area cordoned-off by the emergency services encompassed several blocks. Due to the dangerous structures that needed to be demolished, local businesses, even though unaffected by the original incident, were unable to recover materials from their sites or to serve customers. Several went out of business as the cordon was maintained for six months.*
- *The data centre for one company was located on the first floor above the kitchen of a pizza parlour. The main computer was in fact directly above the cooking ranges. The only exit stairs from the data centre also went through the kitchen.*
- *Company X purchased a site to develop as a dark site, a location where their mainframe computer systems would be. The systems were largely unattended and operated from a control bridge at head office many kilometres distant. There were therefore several risks to this site and the company made the decision not to advertise who owned the site.*

Unfortunately no one mentioned this to the seller's agents who put up a 'sold to company X' board.

- *A subsequent incident at this same site showed that the electronic systems had been designed by the systems' contractors to fail 'safe'. To fail safe meant no one got trapped inside. Unfortunately for company X this also meant that all the security systems switched off and the doors and gates were unlocked.*

Apart from commiserating with company X, these examples highlight the range of risks that can occur and particularly that what may be a good recovery model in one way, can lead to problems in another direction. It is for this reason (and others) that real testing of continuity plans has to be undertaken. Desk checking is just not thorough enough.

Another point to emphasize is that the smaller the business, the more likely an incident is to prove fatal to the business. This is due to the lack of alternative options open to a smaller business. For example they cannot quickly change their business model. They are also less likely to have the cash flow to support extended operation without money coming in. Unfortunately, they are also less likely to have invested in a robust recovery plan due to the cost of that process.

Each organization needs to consider what exactly it is that makes a risk materialize and when the impact of that risk becomes an issue. These aspects will vary between organizations and it is said that one man's risk is another man's opportunity.

Performance evaluation and monitoring

ISO 22301 identifies the need for business continuity to be managed, monitored and reviewed. The onus for this starts with top management and works down, ensuring that everyone in the organization is aware of their responsibilities for and within the business continuity framework. As part of this process, there is a need to document events and issues so that there is a clear record of what has happened and how it has been handled.

Conversely, there is also a need to document events that haven't happened and issues that have been considered but not pursued. All of these aspects are considered further in the following chapters.

PDCA model

ISO 22301 applies the 'Plan–Do–Check–Act' (PDCA) model to planning, establishing, implementing, operating, monitoring, reviewing, maintaining and continually improving the effectiveness of an organization's BCMS.

This ensures a degree of consistency with other management systems standards and thereby supports consistent and integrated implementation and operation with related management systems such as:

- ISO 9001;
- ISO 14001;
- ISO/IEC 20000-1;
- ISO/IEC 27001;
- ISO 28000.

The relationship to the PDCA model and the issues discussed in each section are highlighted at the beginning of each chapter.

The PDCA model itself is discussed further in Chapter 3 and Appendix 3.

2

Setting the business continuity management policy

Setting the scene

Top and senior management are responsible for setting the policies and strategies for the organization. This situation is also true for business continuity and this chapter discusses the issues.

References

ISO 22301, clauses 4.3.1, 4.3.2, 5.2, 5.3, 5.4.

PDCA model

This chapter forms part of the Plan (establish) phase of the business continuity life cycle.

Establish business continuity policy, objectives, targets, controls, processes and procedures relevant to improving business continuity in order to deliver results that align with the organization's overall policies and objectives.

Introduction

The main purpose of a business continuity policy is to direct the organization's overall strategy in respect of business function recovery. It achieves this by:

- establishing the direction and focus of the organization and its business activities;
- identifying how this direction and focus may change over defined periods of time;
- setting any parameters for how the business continuity programme will be implemented.

The approach that is recommended in ISO 22301 to building an effective business continuity programme is to first institute a business continuity management system (BCMS). Essentially this is a formal model that imposes a methodology on the various steps that are necessary to build an effective, appropriate and fully functioning, business continuity plan.

Top management needs to demonstrate its commitment to this process by:

- ensuring that the BCMS is compatible with the strategic direction of the organization;
- integrating the BCMS requirements into the organization's business processes;
- providing the resources to establish, implement, operate, monitor, review and improve the BCMS;
- communicating the importance of effective business continuity management and of conforming to the BCMS requirements;
- ensuring that the BCMS achieves its expected outcomes;
- directing and supporting continual improvement.

It is essential that top management is, and remains, committed to the business continuity project. Auditors from more than one organization have indicated that their top management should put business continuity on the agenda, only to see it lose its place at the front of the queue as the next headline risk appeared in the papers.

Business continuity scope

Once top management has decided to undertake a project to establish a BCMS it needs to define the parameters and scope for this project. This includes identifying the key business functions, products and services that need to be maintained in order for the organization to continue in business.

Typical management considerations will include the following.

- What are the objectives of the organization?
- How are the business objectives of the organization achieved?
- Will the business continuity strategy encompass the whole organization or only parts of it?
- Will the strategy cover the key business areas and functions that support them?
- Is the organization dependent upon others for delivery of its business services?
- Are there other interested parties who should be involved?
- Are there any relevant legal or regulatory issues to consider?
- Is the organization too big, or too diverse, for one strategy to be appropriate?
- What is the timescale in which this project will deliver?
- Should this be an in-house project or outsourced?
- Who, in the organization, will be responsible for the project?
- What sort of budget is envisaged?
- How will top management be updated on progress?

Top management will be aware of most of these issues and the way they wish them to be handled, but some (e.g. costs) may have to wait for the project team to make some progress into how the process will work and the level of outsourcing (if any) required. Top management is likely, however, to look for a broad 'guesstimate' of costs to enable the organization to have some figure for budgeting and financial reporting purposes.

Top management is also unlikely to be fully aware of all the connections that the organization has with other players, such as suppliers, trade organizations, media and regulators. These aspects will have to be pursued and researched by the project team.

The agreed answers to these questions are likely to form the basis for the brief for the project team, and will act as guidance to how the team is set up and the project develops. This brief will form the basis of the business continuity policy.

Audit view

These initial thoughts by top management are very important in an audit perspective, as they will establish the basic framework, including both the opportunities and the constraints of the project. Consequently they could have a major impact upon the final deliverable – the business continuity plan.

In view of this, internal audit needs to be aware of this policy brief and be able to have input to how the project is structured. There is no intention that internal audit should contradict top management or even be on the project team, but it can be very beneficial if there is a process to ensure that internal audit can contribute to the policy brief or awareness of project team members at an early stage.

The purpose of early audit intervention is to ensure that:

- the project is run openly and transparently;
- the project team is aware of its wider responsibilities to the organization and to statutory and other external guidance;
- the project team is aware of the contribution that internal audit, as an independent function within the organization, can bring if required.

Internal audit would normally also have access to minutes from top management meetings and be aware of their briefing for this project and their expectations.

Recovery considerations

Clearly it is the responsibility of top management to determine what level of business continuity is in place and this will be one of the first issues to consider. Recovery considerations will include the following:

How quickly must the business be recovered?

In most organizations the pressure will be on to recover the business as fast as possible in order to maintain customer service and retain cash flow. In some sectors, however, there are external pressures such as having to recover the business within a set number of days or hours in order to satisfy rules, regulations and statutory obligations. A recovery time objective therefore needs to be set for each business function.

How much of the business needs to be recovered on day 1, day 2 and so on?

No established organization came into being on its first trading day with all its present systems, functions and staff in place. Each organization has grown to its current shape and size through an organic process driven by market need, investment, resources and other factors such as regulation. This means that it is highly unlikely that the whole organization needs to be recovered immediately after an incident. The organization can therefore be recovered gradually but, like the well-known 'chicken and egg' situation, someone must determine what comes first.

The decision may be informed by the maximum tolerable period of disruption for each business function. This is the length of time that a business function can continue working in a reduced state. For example, no high street retail shop can trade for long without customers so any recovery plan that did not bring customers in through the door within a few days would not be viable.

What level of risk will be tolerated before the plan comes into effect?

If the previous consideration was the 'chicken and the egg' then this is the 'how long is a piece of string?' question.

As discussed in Chapter 1, management may have different levels of risk appetite according to the nature of the risk and the business function involved.

These decisions therefore need to be established for each business function, as they may differ according to need and intention.

How much input should top management have to the process?

For most projects top management is content to delegate the responsibility to a line function to oversee on its behalf. Business continuity is, however, considerably more significant than many other projects and top management may wish to keep a very close eye on it. Having a senior manager as a member who is directly involved with the project would achieve that.

Most projects report through a steering committee and it would be appropriate for a senior manager to sit on, or probably chair, such a committee to achieve this oversight role.

Management will also need to take into account the dependence, or otherwise, of the organization on third parties (like trading partners) or outsourced arrangements. These issues may mean that the organization has to work with, or rely on, other organizations' business continuity plans to effect a full recovery.

Consideration of these aspects will help to formulate the scope and objectives for the project.

Audit view

While top management will probably wish to recover as much of the business as is possible, audit may be more pragmatic, looking more at the contribution of each business function to the overall organization.

A balanced recovery programme may be a useful option if more than one business function is affected as a result of the incident. For example, loss of a main building will probably affect both back-office and customer-facing operations. Should both types be recovered at once? Should all of one type be recovered? Or should there be a balance?

Top management decisions in this respect may need to be delicately challenged if the result suggests that the organization will fail to achieve the recovery or will face other issues, such as higher costs or a longer recovery period, by pursuing their preferred recovery approach.

Audit should also ensure that the organization's policy brief reflects the responsibilities of the organization and its third parties or outsourcer(s). To do this, audit may need to consult with these external organizations. Ideally this should be enabled through the service contracts, but otherwise it may be necessary to work through senior management to obtain this information.

Partial roll-out

When implementing business continuity policy senior management would expect to decide the extent of this policy and whether it applies to the entire organization or only to parts of it. If it applied to parts of the organization, would it then be extended to the remainder of the organization in due course?

The reasons for a partial or incomplete roll-out might include:

- having a planned and structured continuity roll-out programme that addressed the highest risk business operations first before moving on;
- geographically diverse operations with different risks;
- discrete business units with little or no interdependence with other parts of the organization;
- insufficient resources to institute and implement a full organization-wide recovery programme;
- perceived low risk, or inbuilt mitigation strategies, within some business functions meaning that a continuity programme would not be cost-effective;
- business operations that are nearing the end of their life and where an incident would result in closure rather than recovery.

Any business continuity programme should be subject to change depending upon the way the business develops and evolves. This means that the scope should be under constant review and senior management alerted whenever changes are recommended.

Audit view

Internal audit should have a very good background in the risks faced by the organization and should therefore, almost instinctively, be looking at the scope of the business continuity roll-out against its knowledge of where problems could occur. If the roll-out is a partial one and if the areas covered do not fit with those, audit would then expect some serious questions to be asked. Audit would be looking for a reasonable and defensible justification for omitting higher risk areas from the initial recovery solutions.

Ideally audit should also be looking at producing a matrix analysing the decisions taken. Table 1 provides the framework for such a matrix and highlights the type of issues that need to be captured.

Table 1 Sample policy scope decision matrix

Business function	Terminate risk	Treat risk	Transfer risk	Tolerate risk
Accounts				Implement full business continuity programme immediately
Distribution			Outsource to bring risks into one place	
Warehousing				No changes planned as risk reduction already undertaken
Retail shops – city centre		Initiate risk reduction review followed by continuity strategy by year end		
Retail shops – out of town centres		Initiate risk reduction review followed by continuity strategy mid next year		
Retail shops – small communities	Consider sale of premises as opportunity presents to reduce geographic spread and distribution costs			

NOTE: This document would form the index to a more detailed review and consideration of the issues and findings identified.

Once the organization has built up experience with undertaking the data collection, risk analysis and plan development that will be required for a partial roll-out, it may find that it is easier to continue the roll-out across a wider area. Indeed, the data collection exercise may have captured significant data that would be directly usable in a wider roll-out. Internal audit therefore needs to bear in mind the amount of work already undertaken but not being utilized when it considers whether the scope of the business continuity policy is appropriate.

Organizational strategy

The business continuity process should be aligned to the organization's strategy to ensure that it:

- embodies the direction and focus of the business and ensures that the business impact and risk assessment activities are appropriate and thorough;
- understands the way the organization expects to change its business plan over future periods to enable the business continuity programme to better reflect present and future needs and to ensure flexibility is retained;
- establishes the maximum geographical extent of a disruption or the extent of a resource loss that the organization needs to plan to survive and recover from.

Organizations may find that they need more than one business continuity strategy to cope with different business aspects or significant differences in working locations or arrangements. If this is the case then the need for these should be clearly spelt out to ensure that the project team is working in the right direction.

Audit view

While top management will be setting the project parameters and the breadth of the project, there are some matters, such as the organization's strategy, which may present a problem. This is because, although there is a stated and promulgated organizational strategy, management may be contemplating changes or significant actions that could have an impact upon this. Naturally they may not wish to publicize their thinking too early as this could cause other problems, but to send the business continuity project off in inappropriate directions could lead to the continuity plan and reality diverging in the future.

Internal audit should be aware of the potential conflict that could arise and take appropriate steps to obtain management commitment to, at least, a set of statements that enable the business continuity project team to build their plans without fear that imminent business changes will render them obsolete. Audit are well placed to act in this way as they need to be close to senior management decisions in order to focus their general work on providing the reassurances that management need.

Policy content

The structure of the business continuity policy will differ between organizations and will also depend on whether top management has already decided to retain the project in-house or to outsource it. It is not essential for management to make such a decision at this stage. It may choose instead to reconsider this option after an internal project team has carried out some preliminary work, perhaps to ascertain workload, costs and so on.

If the option is taken for an outsourced solution the policy document will need to be detailed and be accompanied by other supporting information describing the organization, including its business focus and its aspirations and aims. Together, this brief will effectively form an invitation to tender that will allow the tendering organization to assess the work required and bid accordingly.

The business continuity policy outline from top management needs to:

- be appropriate to the purpose of the organization;
- provide the framework for setting business continuity objectives;
- include a commitment to satisfy applicable requirements;
- include a commitment to continual improvement of the BCMS;
- be communicated within the organization to all persons working for or on behalf of the organization within the scope of the BCMS;
- be reviewed for continuing suitability at defined intervals and when significant changes occur;
- be available to interested parties, as appropriate and as approved by management.

A normal in-house policy brief is likely to include the following:

Introduction

This section explains the aims of the policy and any necessary framework on which it is built. In a large and mature organization there may be no need for an introduction, but in smaller organizations the policy may set out the background to, and importance of, business continuity planning.

Scope

This section provides statements on what the organization expects to achieve from a business continuity plan and who will be affected within the organization. These statements will form the criteria against which the effectiveness of the policy and the project on which it is based can later be audited and judged.

Responsibilities

This will define the initial roles and responsibilities of the project team.

The project team will develop other roles and responsibilities within the business continuity plan as the plan takes shape.

Deliverables

This section will lay down the key aspects that need to be achieved. Essentially it will also ensure that top management retains control of the project.

It is likely that this section will be written at a high level but will include:

- a definition of business continuity;
- an operational framework to show management the key stages of the project with responsibilities, decision points, milestones and any sign-off activities;
- a requirement for the project team to identify any relevant standards, regulations and legislation that must be considered while developing a business continuity policy. Also to identify any relevant sector guidelines or 'best practice' examples from other organizations that could be used;

- a need to identify and document the components necessary for a business continuity policy;
- a requirement for any output to conform to organizational standards and requirements;
- a stipulation that the business continuity plan drafts are widely consulted on, including by top management, and that only they may sign off the final version;
- a requirement that once the business continuity plan is approved it may be published and promulgated throughout the organization;
- an obligation for the project team to put in place a maintenance process to ensure the business continuity plan is kept up to date and a document management system to ensure that only the latest version of the plan is in use.

If the organization already has a business continuity plan in place, perhaps as part of a division or subsidiary, then there may be a need for a 'gap analysis' of that plan to determine where strengths and weaknesses lie and whether any changes need to be made to it.

To ensure that the policy covers the needs of key business functions, management may consult with those functions while the plan is still in draft form to enable their views to be captured.

Audit view

As with any policy, care needs to be taken in ensuring that it expresses what is meant and is not made up of a series of statements that cannot be effectively implemented or measured.

When reviewing the policy brief audit should consider whether it meets the test of having SMART objectives. The concept behind this approach is shown in Table 2.

Given that this policy will form the basis of all the future work undertaken in the organization on business continuity, it needs to be well researched and considered. Internal audit should therefore review it at the earliest opportunity and plan a formal review, if not before the release of the consultation draft then immediately after, and try to ensure that the final version is not released until the audit is completed.

Table 2 SMART objectives

Acronym	Meaning
Specific	The policy states precisely what is to be achieved.
Measurable	The objectives of the policy can be clearly seen and measured.
Achievable	The objectives of the policy are feasible given the organization's resources and capabilities.
Relevant	The objectives of the policy are important to the organization and achievable by those tasked with them.
Time-bound	Any start and end dates are clearly stated and defined.

The audit criteria will centre on the policy deliverables, but will also consider all the other aspects identified as part of, or contributing to, the policy contents.

Where an organization goes down a more relaxed route by having little written guidance for the project team, audit should ensure that the project team develops its own guidance and then goes back to top management to get this signed off.

Internal or external project team?

Having established the policy it is likely that senior management will determine who should undertake the project. This could be an in-house business function, an outsourced provider or a mix of the two to provide a co-sourced solution.

There are several reasons for selecting an external provider.

- Existing business operations are not greatly impacted by the project as no key staff are involved.
- There is no in-house learning curve.
- External suppliers may be very experienced in this area and management may feel that their professionalism and knowledge would be vital in achieving a faster result.
- The organization needs the plan up and running as soon as possible and there may be an opportunity to speed up the process by using specialists who have built these plans before.

In-house developed solutions, however, offer the following advantages.

- Undertaking the research involves analysing systems and processes. This can lead to business process improvements to the long-term benefit of the organization.
- Staff become involved in the process and work with it.
- With no big cheques to sign it appears to be a cheaper process. There are, however, several offsetting issues that may work against this assumption.
- In-house systems are not exposed to external gaze. From a security perspective it may be better to keep knowledge of in-house systems within the organization.

Equally, this decision brings with it the potential for some key disadvantages, as follows.

- An outsourced solution will have to work harder to obtain buy-in across the business. Staff may adopt the view that if they are not needed in developing the process, they are not needed in implementing it either.
- An in-house team may be 'persuaded' by strong managers to put those managers' interests ahead of those of the organization. This is especially true if the team, or its members, relies on one or more of those managers for bonuses, career enhancements or other work-related aspects.

The one key tenet that must be remembered as part of this decision is: *you can outsource the problem, but you cannot outsource the risk.*

Outsourcing does not remove any responsibilities for the process. These remain with the organization, and there is also the need to manage the outsourcer. The main advantage of outsourcing is that all the risks can be packaged neatly in one place at a cost that is known and accepted. The primary downside is that the outsourcing may be transparent to the customer and the organization will still face reputation risk issues if anything goes wrong.

Audit view

Selecting either option is an operational decision. Internal audit should therefore only review the decision along with the justifications and assumptions made in reaching that decision.

If an outsourcer is used audit should ensure that the contract between the organization and the outsourcer allows audit access to the systems, processes and functions that are to be used to support the organization. This is to enable audit to undertake reviews of specific aspects of the outsourced activities, as well as full end-to-end reviews spanning both organizations.

In-house project

If top management opts for an in-house project team there are several business functions that have a vested interest in business continuity, such as:

- security;
- facilities;
- information systems.

There is no right answer to whether any particular business function should lead such a project. It is, however, better to employ a dedicated person who is self-motivated and has an ability to achieve. The team will probably be cross-functional anyway to provide a good mix of skills and this will help alleviate the effect of the project on the staffing resources of the organization.

There is considerable advantage in choosing a person who is trained and experienced in business continuity. Such a person would be able to determine problem areas and weaknesses before they progressed too far or were incorporated in the plan. They would also be able to draw upon their experience to ensure that other team members were of the right calibre to be involved in the project. It would also enhance the organization and the credibility of the project team to have an experienced professional in charge.

As discussed in Chapter 1, internal audit, as a function, cannot run such a project in its own right. It can be involved in the project, and should be, but it is not able to make the operational decisions that would need to be made. To do so would compromise its independence. A specific internal auditor who has the right skills may perhaps be chosen as project manager, but this would have to be on a consultancy engagement with a specific contract in place for this job.

There are governance rules in place to ensure that external audit does not run any in-house project, although, as with internal auditors, there is little to prevent an external audit company offering a consultancy contract to run such a project.

Audit view

Although internal audit cannot run such a project, it needs to be involved as soon as possible.

A common management view is that internal audit is there to look at a project 'after the event', and in some cases that is a valid view. Business continuity is, however, a long process with many opportunities for operational decisions along the way. The problem with leaving internal audit to come in at the end is that time has been lost and decisions may, by then, be cast in stone, leaving the organization with long-term problems.

A true story may illustrate this:

In the mid-1990s a financial institution decided to initiate a business continuity plan. The requirement was that the business should be recoverable in 3 days (72 hours). The organization operated under a strong code of conduct and failure to recover in that time period would mean that it would be taken over.

Among its 3,000-plus staff was a middle-ranking employee who was interested in the subject and volunteered to take on the project. He was given the task, the time, and many months later, someone to help him. He estimated the project would take 12 months.

He progressed around the organization interviewing manager after manager. He found that many of these managers had things in common:

- *they overestimated the importance of their section or department in the organization's recovery plan;*
- *they needed provision for more staff and more resources in the recovery plan than they currently had even though their recovery workload did not justify this;*
- *they insisted on knowing exactly where they would be recovered to (building, room number and so on). The concept of an 'unpredictable' incident or disaster was lost on them.*

He went on also to discover that senior management itself did not really know what the appropriate recovery sequence should be.

The IT function tested its disaster recovery processes regularly (although never to the extent of actually relocating the live system). They improved these processes as needed and could, in theory, easily meet the 72-hour rule.

Approximately 30 months after he started, he presented his final report along with the business continuity plans and left the organization.

Reports to top management had been positive so an internal audit review was not held until some time after his departure.

When the review took place it showed that the organization would not recover in 72 hours. In fact, using his plan, it would no longer even recover its basic IT functions within that time period. Further, it showed that things were recovered out of sequence, such as the electronic mail system being restored after it was needed to provide business communication facilities.

Other issues also came to light, including that the local roads were not wide enough at the primary recovery location to cope with the trucks that were scheduled to bring in the temporary accommodation for displaced staff.

Consequently the plan was scrapped and a new continuity planning process started immediately. By the time a workable plan was implemented the organization had lost almost four years since it started. Considerable effort from many contributors had been wasted and the organization remained under threat of takeover if any major incident had occurred.

Other issues that may go wrong include:

- the organization goes off on its own without considering lessons learnt elsewhere;
- top management approves the project and then turns its attention elsewhere and does not oversee it properly;
- the project team is not strong enough to deal with some of the individuals involved;
- the costs of the project in terms of time and resource are not appreciated and not budgeted for;
- the whole project simply runs out of steam.

The involvement of internal audit early in the project is therefore not difficult to justify. What is difficult to justify, however, is *not* involving internal audit.

Staff policy statement

Once a business continuity management programme is underway, top management may consider the need to bring all staff on board. One way to do this is to prepare and promulgate a business continuity policy statement for all staff. This would rank alongside the security policy, data protection policy and other similar documents.

As opposed to the document issued to the project team, the staff policy statement would focus on the issues that staff would need to know in order to facilitate or become involved in business continuity.

Although this policy statement is usefully issued at the time of the decision to develop a business continuity management programme, this is not necessary and in many cases it will not be issued until the business continuity plan is actually in place. This type of policy is therefore considered further in Appendix 7, along with a full discussion on auditing such a policy statement.

Performance monitoring and evaluation

As part of its commitment to the development process, top management needs to ensure that there are processes in place to capture any data that may be needed for record purposes as well as for future checking. Apart from the brief given to the project team, data of this type will include how interested parties' needs have been considered. Such parties will include:

- customers;
- investors;
- shareholders;
- the supply chain;
- the public;
- the local community.

Management may of course brief the project team to deal with these aspects but they do need to have communicated a view on how closely these others should be involved or consulted.

The other key aspect that management needs to ensure is included in the retained documentation is clear records of what is to be excluded from the plans and why. The perceptions that management operate under today may be widely different from those in a few months' or years' time and their successors may therefore need to understand why certain aspects have been omitted from the plans.

Audit view

Internal audit can only support this approach. The more that is recorded and retained of the thinking behind the project, the easier it will be in the future to determine if the project has been successful. Similarly, the reasoning behind decisions, especially exclusions or prioritizing one aspect over another will be of major importance as the organization develops and changes in the future.

3

Developing the business continuity programme

Setting the scene

With the business continuity policy established, the organization has a defined direction for implementing the processes it needs to ensure the outcome it wants. This chapter looks at the requirements of this business continuity management programme and how it can become part of a sustainable life cycle process.

References

ISO 22301 clauses: 4.2.1, 4.2.2, 4.4, 7.2, 7.5.1, 7.5.2, 7.5.3, 9.1.1, 9.1.2, 9.3, 10.2.

PDCA model

This chapter forms part of the Plan (establish) phase of the business continuity life cycle.

Establish business continuity policy, objectives, targets, controls, processes and procedures relevant to improving business continuity in order to deliver results that align with the organization's overall policies and objectives.

Introduction

A business continuity management system (BCMS) does not spring into being overnight. It requires a great deal of planning to ensure that it meets the needs of the organization and its various business functions. There are several ways to ensure that this happens but the most usual is to use the policy brief prepared by top management as a basic building block for a formal project.

A structured project then enables the organization to look at what it needs, what best practice and experience offers, and to meld the two views to form a workable solution. To ensure it remains up to date there needs to be feedback into the process from ongoing activities, future business changes, results of testing, user concerns and so on. In essence therefore a complete life cycle needs to be recognized and planned for to enable a sustainable and usable business continuity management system to be developed.

Business continuity life cycle

It is essential that any business continuity programme established gains the commitment of the organization's senior management. Once the programme is developed it needs to incorporate self-management and regular updating processes to ensure that it remains current and usable.

Establishing a systems life cycle to ensure that the business continuity programme is introduced, developed and managed through its life is a useful approach to adopt, as it enables an organization to control the processes better and understand what is involved at each stage.

ISO 22301 applies the 'Plan–Do–Check–Act' (PDCA) model to planning, establishing, implementing, operating, monitoring, reviewing, maintaining and continually improving the effectiveness of the organization's BCMS.

Figure 3 reproduced from ISO 22301 illustrates how a BCMS takes as inputs interested parties, requirements for continuity management and, through the necessary actions and processes, produces a managed business continuity process that meets those input requirements.

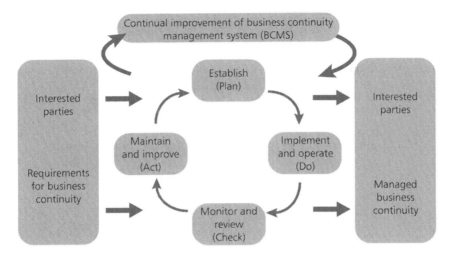

Figure 3 The PDCA cycle for business continuity

ISO 22301 defines the individual steps of the process in the following way:

Plan (Establish)

Establish business continuity policy, objectives, targets, controls, processes and procedures relevant to managing risk and to improving business continuity in order to deliver results that align with the organization's overall policies and objectives.

Do (Implement and operate)

Implement and operate the business continuity policy, controls, processes and procedures.

Check (Monitor and review)

Monitor and review performance against business continuity policy and objectives, report the results to management for review, and determine and authorize actions for remediation and improvement.

Act (Maintain and improve)

Maintain and improve the BCMS by taking corrective action, based on the results of management review and reappraising the scope of the BCMS and business continuity policy and objectives.

A fuller discussion of system life cycle management is in Appendix 3.

Audit view

Establishing a life cycle methodology for the business continuity project involves assigning responsibility for each phase of the cycle so that the overall process progresses smoothly and accurately. Ideally, internal audit needs to be involved at each of the stages.

An audit programme should be established to formalize the way these cycle phases are to be reviewed. A sample programme is also included in Appendix 3.

Implementing business continuity management

As the development of a business continuity plan is essentially a project, it needs a clear executive mandate to ensure commitment and cooperation from those involved in providing information and implementing the plan's provisions.

It needs to be appreciated that businesses seldom function alone and there will be a certain degree of interdependence between the organization and its trading partners, suppliers and others. These relationships need to be reflected in the continuity planning approach as well as in the final plan. This may mean the project team works with similar project teams in its trading partners and suppliers.

Except in very small organizations where the owner or manager may end up doing all the work, such decisions are usually made at top management level and delegated down through the organization to achieve the desired outcomes. Senior managements in these larger organizations therefore need to have a clear vision of what they are trying to achieve and what resources they will apply to the tasks involved.

While this book talks about having a project team to develop the business continuity plan, this may not be the appropriate structure in every organization. The smaller the organization, the smaller the number of people that is likely to be involved. It should be noted, however, that no single person should be given the remit to develop the whole continuity plan. Partly this is due to the amount of work involved and therefore the time the project will take but, most importantly, no one person can envisage all the issues, problems and opportunities developing the plan will entail or treat them all as objectively as they need.

Top management, however, needs to maintain a strong connection with the project, ideally by appointing one of their members to be involved at a high level and to report back to them on progress. Having senior management representation on the steering board of a project like this will also ensure that issues like resourcing and work priorities will be quickly resolved.

Audit view

Most incidents can be considered to have four stages:

- the initial response;
- the consolidation phase;
- the recovery phase;
- the restoration of normality.

An investigation into the cause of the incident, together with the attendant hearings, may be superimposed onto the whole structure.

Internal audit needs to reassure itself, and management, that the business continuity management programme will deliver the components and processes needed to address these stages.

Establishing a project to develop the continuity programme provides a positive indication of top management's intent and also sends a clear signal through the rest of the organization of the importance of business continuity planning.

It also provides audit with an opportunity to look at the decision and its justifications and assumptions as part of reviewing top management's activities. Not all audit functions review their senior management, but technically there is nothing to prevent this. Top management should in fact welcome the scrutiny, as it ensures good governance – something that is increasingly under the microscope.

The policy brief, once approved, will then form the basis of the project's remit.

A useful scope for an audit is *to ensure that planning appropriately meets the requirements of the business.*

Establishing the project

A formal project is less likely to be derailed by other considerations than an informal arrangement. It will also have a number of distinct phases and these, along with the audit issues involved, are discussed in Appendix 4.

Where the organization is small the roles of project manager and project team members may be more blurred and the whole business continuity programme may perhaps be left to one person. In such cases, the principles identified above should be observed where possible, but it is accepted that this is more difficult.

The key tenets are to:

- pick the person who leads the project wisely. Smaller organizations need people who can succeed rather than those who won't fail;
- impose job separation wherever possible. This is to ensure that key decisions (e.g. spending, eliminating controls and accepting risks) have to be vetted;
- ensure that the project is run to the benefit of the organization. Running any project to 'tick boxes' is not beneficial, there must be clear gains for any price paid.

However the process is to be managed, whether through a project or otherwise, top management should assign roles and responsibilities to the key players, or at least the lead person (project manager), early on in the process. This provides for transparency in who is doing what and the accountability for actions taken. Assignment of roles should be backed by the provision, or amendment, of job profiles for the staff and managers involved and these will also act as a measure against which subsequent actions can be objectively judged.

Audit view

The audit effort should be focused on the key parts of the project to ensure that the organization is going to obtain best advantage from its investment in this project. Nevertheless, the selection of project manager and the choice of in-house or outsourced solution are of paramount interest and need to be vetted.

Where the project team is small or only comprises one person, there should be a greater audit review presence to ensure that there is no personal bias or subjectivity built into the project, and that there is clear separation in key areas such as financial control.

Internal audit will wish to ensure that the organization has taken appropriate steps to:

- determine the necessary competence of person(s) doing work under its control that affects its performance;
- ensure these persons are competent on the basis of appropriate education, training and experience;
- take actions, where necessary, to ensure these persons acquire the necessary competence;
- evaluate the effectiveness of any training provided or any other support provided to give staff the appropriate competence;
- retain appropriate documented information as evidence of competence and any actions taken.

These issues could therefore usefully form the basis of an audit scope.

Project manager

The project manager is a key person in the development of a BCMS, as it will be their responsibility to:

- promote the project;
- work and consult with all levels of staff and management within the organization;
- work with external parties and perhaps outsourcers;
- liaise with emergency and other services;
- successfully manage people, time and budget;
- develop solutions to problems and issues;
- motivate the project team;
- produce an appropriate plan;
- bring the project in on time and on budget.

The person chosen is likely to have experience of project management and/ or have skills in the business continuity arena. If they are not skilled in business continuity or project management then some form of training may be appropriate.

As explained in Chapter 1, an internal audit team member could sit on the project team as project manager, or other key role, but only if top management had established a separate contract with that audit team member to specifically act in that capacity. The contract would need to specify the role, responsibilities and duration of the contract. Such a contract would ensure that the internal audit team member was working as a 'consultant' for the organization during that period rather than as a member of internal audit. Top management might choose to do this if an audit team member had specific skills that could be useful or essential in such a project (e.g. prior experience running such a project).

The project manager is likely to be appointed on a full-time basis and have a suitable job description. If it is a part-time post, their existing job description should be amended to reflect this additional role and its responsibilities. The job description would normally stem from management's requirements for the project.

For an organization short of project and business continuity skills there is always the option to recruit a suitable candidate to join the organization specifically to run the project. Clearly this is not a route available to those needing to build their plans in a hurry.

Audit view

The person chosen to head the project says much about management's intentions towards the project itself.

Internal audit may therefore wish to open a discussion with top management early to ensure that a respected, recognized and successful person is given the task. If the organization chooses to recruit for the project manager role then audit may consider sitting in on the recruitment process to contribute to the views on candidates' suitability.

The job description should be reviewed as part of a governance audit to ensure that it appropriately reflects the requirements of the organization while not expecting the individual to enter into any conflicts of interest or operate beyond the law in any way.

The project team

While internal auditors are often involved as part-time members of the project team, it would be more unusual to see them seconded to that role in a full-time capacity. This usually has more to do with audit priorities than any other consideration. Nevertheless, even a part-time presence can provide big gains in enabling the project team to obtain advice and validation on risk, control matters and decisions quickly and easily.

Members of the project team should have job descriptions for the role they are carrying out. Often it will be the project manager who is responsible for drafting these based on the needs of the project.

Where necessary, members of the project team should have appropriate training to ensure they can perform the tasks expected of them.

Audit view

Being involved with the project from the early stages holds significant benefits both for internal audit and for the organization.

For the project the main benefit is that internal audit has a wider view and remit than most others in the organization. This means that they can contribute informed views on:

- risks and control issues;
- how parts of the organization are likely to react to specific proposals or operating suggestions;
- what has worked or failed elsewhere;
- suggestions for improvement based on experience and best practice in other organizations;
- monitoring, reviewing and testing all or parts of the project.

Audit benefits are primarily operational in the sense of being aware of the project, having input to it and being able to use it as part of the process for providing management with assurances about the organization's processes and systems.

Training

Training for the business continuity project and subsequent implementation of the plan needs to be considered carefully and built into the project timescales and costs. Although training is an ongoing process it should be specifically considered in the light of the project.

Prior to developing the plan

Training for selected and potential business continuity project team members should ideally begin early. It is possible that the person chosen to be project manager or to coordinate development of the plan may have undergone formal, professional and/or certification training.

If this is the case then this person should train members of the project team as necessary to enable them to perform their tasks more efficiently. If the project lead time is long enough then these team members may instead undertake their own formal training.

If there is no trained or experienced person in the team then the organization should consider whether this is an aspect that needs to be resolved before the project progresses.

After developing the plan

Once the business continuity plan has been developed and implemented it will be advantageous to transfer the team's knowledge of the continuity process, as well as the plan and its background, to those who will be responsible for implementing it.

Similarly, it should be ensured that managers and users in the various business functions undergo training and awareness programmes in the various issues that will involve them. Some may be practical matters like exiting the building, cascading information to their staff and being alert to risks, while other training may be more specific in relation to their role in an incident.

With the plan in place

Testing is the best form of training that is available. Management, project team and staff can all see the effect of the plan and where things can be improved. This will lead to a better plan and better reception and reaction from those outside the project.

Audit view

Business continuity is usually a large budget exercise, but its effects and value can be seriously weakened if there are no training or awareness programmes in place.

Unfortunately training is often one of the first things to be removed from budgets when savings need to be made. This may be a false economy, as untrained staff can cause considerable damage and business disruption.

Internal audit should be challenging management to retain and expand training budgets, especially in areas such as business continuity, where acquired skills can reduce the project timescales, improve the plan and make things work better in the event of an incident.

Audit should also be insisting on testing the plan. The greater and more comprehensive the testing, the more will be learnt and the more effective the plan will be in the event of a real incident. Testing is discussed further in Chapter 8.

Internal audit should also be monitoring commitments made by the organization and ensuring they are dealt with. The following illustrates a typical example.

An audit team highlighted that their organization had put its business continuity strategy on the intranet. This made it clear that the roles of staff would be explained to them by their managers. Several months after that strategy was released, the audit team challenged the director responsible for the project as they had not received any training. The director did not realize that such a commitment had been made.

Inputs to the team

Once the project team begins to take shape it will need to ensure that it receives material that is relevant and appropriate to its defined task.

Its first input will be from top management defining its role. After that it will need to start monitoring the organization to determine what is happening. This involves monitoring:

- what directions are being taken;
- what are the key issues;
- what are the key risks;
- whether there is there any relevant legislation;
- who should be involved from outside the organization;
- any changes that are planned.

Much of this information will come from the experience of the project team members. From their knowledge of the organization they will also know where to obtain the information that they need and will forge contacts as necessary. This is one of the most difficult aspects in an outsourced project, as the incoming project team are unlikely to have much, if any, awareness of the way the organization operates, who are the key players and where information is available.

As the team members start the interviews and begin to build up their own documentation they will begin to see the patterns and parameters of the task.

One of the primary pieces of documentation built up during the interview stages is the business impact analysis. This is dealt with more fully in Chapter 4, but in essence is a statement of the impact that disruption might cause on systems and processes within the organization. Clearly the business impact analysis documents are very important and any changes to these, perhaps due to system or business direction updates and/or the risks they face, need to be fed back into the project. This will help ensure that the project remains focused in the right direction.

Audit view

All teams start the project with their own preconceived ideas. It is essential that internal audit is in a position to challenge these views and to ensure that the views and directions taken by the team are objective and based on fact and not myth.

It should not be overlooked that much of the information within an organization is not written down but is tacit information held in the memory of those who work there. Often this knowledge will have been built up over many years and may hold the key to why an organization performs a task a certain way, or has other specific processes. Capturing this information is clearly much harder than locating paper-based or electronically held records. In this area there is no substitute for interviews and working closely with those who really do understand the organization.

For the much larger enterprise there is software available that will capture information in various forms, such as images and speech, and turn it into documents. Likewise documents and other material that are not in standard formats can be captured and turned into usable documents. These processes of capturing unstructured information are leading to organizations holding an increasing amount of information that is readily accessible to use, view or analyse.

Outsourcing the project

Rather than build an in-house team to tackle the issue of developing a business continuity management strategy, management may decide to outsource the project.

In this event there will still need to be a project manager or liaison officer within the organization to ensure that the outsourcer provides the contracted service and meets the needs of top management and the organization. This again is a key role but it is more likely to require people skills than project management ones.

It is important that there is one recognized link to the outsourcer and this person should be the only one who has the authority to deliver decisions on the project or amend any deliverable, milestone or other key aspect of the project. This is essential, as otherwise the organization could find that any number of staff or managers are involved and perhaps giving conflicting advice, or requesting work that is not in the contract terms.

Any outsourcing arrangement should be subject to a contract that determines what the outsourcer must undertake and deliver. This could be anything from a limited review and partial work on the project, through to complete delivery of a working and tested plan plus ongoing management. The choice lies with the organization and will be decided as much by in-house capabilities and resources as by cost.

There also needs to be a clear understanding between the organization and the outsourcer of any deliverables and responsibilities as well as a set of criteria against which the contract outcomes can be assessed.

One of the deliverables may be for the outsourcer to cross-train internal staff during the project. This transfer of skills will enable the organization to better manage the ongoing maintenance of the programme as well as future changes.

Audit view

Internal audit should review the outsourcing contract as part of its general reviews on contracts and the liabilities that the organization may have accepted. This will also highlight any conditions the outsourced team may have to meet. It may also be worthwhile to ensure that there is no impediment in the contract to internal audit interviewing these contractors or consultants about their role and activities within the business continuity project.

An incoming team will require support to help it find its feet and to understand where the key information sources are held. Audit is in a good position to advise on this.

Audit should also review the links within the organization to ensure that the outsourcer only has a single point of contact.

Steering committee

Whether the organization opts for an in-house project or any degree of outsourcing it is beneficial if there is a steering committee, or project board, established to monitor the project as a whole.

The steering committee would normally be made up of managers drawn from functions across the organization. Ideally it should also include a representative of top management and normally they would chair this committee.

A possible membership list could include the following individuals.

- Senior management or executive sponsor who has overall responsibility for business continuity. This person would normally seek senior management's support and direction as well as ensuring that adequate resourcing and funding is available for the project. They are most likely to chair the meetings as well.
- The project manager. This person would work with senior management and estimate funding and resource requirements. Their role would also include coordinating and overseeing the business impact analysis; ensuring effective participant input; coordinating and overseeing the development of plans and arrangements for business continuity; establishing working groups and teams and defining their responsibilities; coordinating appropriate training; and providing for regular review, testing and audit of the plans and process.
- The organization's security officer. Their role would be to work with the project manager to ensure that all aspects of the continuity plan meet the security requirements of the organization.
- Chief information officer or head of IT. Their role would be to cooperate closely with the project manager and IT specialists to ensure that there is an effective and harmonized continuity programme.
- Representatives of the business functions. These will provide input to the project, and ensure that the final plans meet their needs and expectations.

The purpose of the steering committee is to oversee the project. This means that it receives progress reports from the project manager and considers actions taken and due against the project plan and the agreed timetable of events. Any proposed changes in the project, its milestones, deliverables or timetable are then discussed and agreed upon.

The steering committee would normally:

- approve the governance structure of the project;
- clarify their roles, and those of participants in the programme;
- oversee the creation, as required, of committees, working groups and teams to develop and execute the plan;
- provide strategic direction and communicate with the project team;
- approve the results of the business impact analysis;
- review the critical services, functions and products that have been identified;
- approve the continuity plans and arrangement;
- monitor quality assurance activities;
- resolve conflicting interests and priorities.

The steering committee will also provide approval for the project spend and authorize additional resources where justified and agreed as necessary. The presence of a senior management member can be invaluable in smoothing the way for requests for additional budget and other resources.

Although an outsourced project would have one point of contact within the organization to deal with it on project matters, it is likely that there will still be a steering committee to monitor and oversee the project. This is because the organization, although outsourcing the project, still has responsibility for it. The primary organizational contact for the outsourcer would be a member or participant in the steering committee.

The steering committee will not sit all the time but will meet at regular intervals. For a business continuity project this is likely to be at approximately monthly intervals depending upon the planned spend of the project, its milestones and the commitments of the committee members.

Audit view

A steering committee is a very useful body, as it has the authority to ask questions and get answers. Its members will also have the experience and knowledge to explore project decisions and progress and to look at potential opportunities that might arise. It is therefore a very useful committee for a senior internal auditor to sit on over and above any other audit presence on the project team.

In the unlikely event that audit is denied a permanent presence on the steering committee, audit might wish to try to gain access as an 'observer'. This will provide the opportunity to monitor the project, although without being able to contribute directly to the debate unless asked. An audit observer can still lobby and discuss issues with committee members outside the meeting if necessary.

Communication with interested parties

Once the project team has been established and has its own terms of reference in place, it should begin to communicate with others within and outside the organization. This will help to establish the project as well as opening information channels and helping to define the project itself.

Although the primary stakeholders contacted will initially be staff, the project team must also link up with trading partners, customers and others (see Figure 4) to ensure that they know what is happening and how it may affect them. Similarly there are regulatory issues that need to be considered as well as business obligations and the various providers of these (such as the emergency services) who will need to be involved as things progress.

Successful implementation of the programme may be communicated to shareholders and the wider public where it is perceived to be of value. Most organizations will not need to do this as they will consider this 'business as usual', but for those where the risks may be higher it could be a worthwhile move.

Audit view

To some extent the effectiveness of the project team can be assessed by how quickly and efficiently it emerges from the business of setting up the project and getting on with collecting, collating and analysing the data.

Although audit should not be slowing down the project team at this time it should still stay aware of what is happening and provide whatever advice and assistance that may be needed.

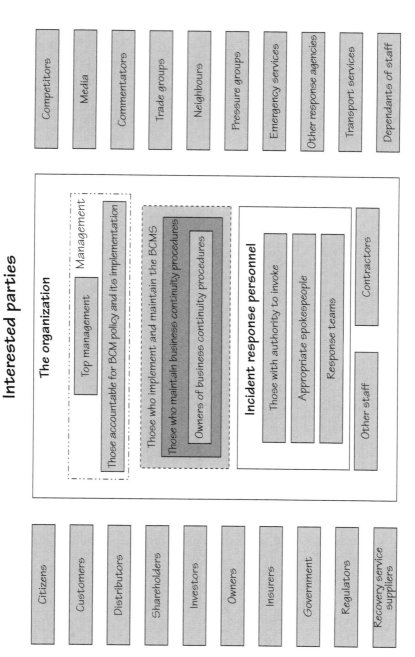

Figure 4 Examples of interested parties to be considered in public and private sectors

One area that audit may have a view on, however, is the publicity that is given to the project. Clearly such information should show the organization in a good light but also it should not enable others to perceive particular weaknesses of the organization that could be exploited.

Performance evaluation and monitoring

Probably in conjunction with the project team, top management will need to determine how the project and subsequent business continuity activities are evaluated and monitored.

This will essentially require understanding of:

- what needs to be measured and monitored;
- the methods for monitoring, measurement, analysis and evaluation to ensure valid results;
- when the monitoring and measuring needs to be performed;
- when the analysis and evaluation of monitoring and measurement results needs to be performed;
- how to react to the results and any problems found.

The project team should already be aware of the criteria for the project and the particular aspects that management places most emphasis upon. In addition to these, they will need to understand both how the health of the business continuity process can be assessed as well as being aware of the changing risks facing the organization. There may also be a number of other areas that they could keep an eye on, including whether the culture of the organization supports the business continuity plan and ensures that staff and contractors are aware of their roles and responsibilities as well as having the tools to discharge those roles effectively.

Monitoring the various issues and aspects may require a range of tools and approaches. Where technology is involved, there may be opportunities to build in continuous monitoring tools that report back at regular intervals or perhaps when specific events occur, such as a particular error number occurring in a program or an event being monitored that is outside its normal parameters such as an air conditioning fault.

However, not all monitoring will be through technology. Security services may use CCTV, radio and paper-based media for their reporting. Staff identifying problems may use the telephone or visit face to face. So the options open to the project team to build systems that will capture and be able to effectively use all the incoming data are quite challenging.

Some of this monitoring will be in the hands of others – for example, it is unlikely that every organization will be monitoring earthquake, weather or flood patterns.

Where monitoring is not continuous, the project team will need to determine when it should happen and how often. For example, how many fire alarm drills should the organization have each year or how often should the water in the hot water tanks and air conditioning systems be checked for Legionnaires' Disease?

Clearly, with something as potentially risky as Legionnaires' Disease, there is likely to be an immediate escalation of the results if it is found, but what is the trigger level when other reports become significant and how often should reports be requested? The project team will need to determine these issues as well as to whom the reports will go.

Audit view

This is always a tricky one and internal audit should always be careful about coming down on a team who have not got all the monitoring in place especially if it only finds out with hindsight what is actually needed. The real key is that there is a structured and logical approach followed to find out what is relevant and how it should be monitored.

The range of aspects to monitor may be huge, depending upon the nature of the organization and what it has identified as a risk to its well-being and continued operation. For example, there will be a range of almost standard risks that include loss of premises, loss of staff, natural hazards and so on. The issue is how might these be triggered and when could the organization spot the trend or increasing risk? As an example, it is worth looking at one category, say loss of premises. The following are some of the main potential threats and their underlying causes.

- loss through inability to pay the rent:
  - financial problem;
  - system problem;
  - legal action.

- loss through landlord action:
  - lease terminated;
  - essential repairs not carried out;
  - legal dispute.
- loss through access being blocked:
  - snow, flood, etc.;
  - infrastructure works such as road repairs;
  - collapse of building;
  - protest group established outside;
  - nearby incident.

As can be seen, some of these are easier to monitor than others. Some fall within the organization's scope to monitor directly and others almost certainly would be outsourced to others to monitor. Remember this is just a very small example of the overall monitoring requirement.

The answer to much of this really lies with where the reports are going. There needs to be sufficient capability to cope with all the inputs, sufficient understanding of the risk attitude to know what these various items of information mean for the organization and sufficient authority to deal appropriately with what is found. If audit can ensure that the project team sets that kind of approach up then the organization will be well on the way to a proper monitoring system.

Documentation

As part of the development of the BCMS, each organization will need to build up a collection of documentation. This information will serve to illustrate why certain decisions have been taken, enable the organization to understand the range of its assets and obligations, and bring together all the key decisions in one place.

The main aspects of this documentation will include:

- policy brief containing scope and terms of reference;
- any aspects that are considered to be outside the scope of the policy;
- legal and regulatory issues that need to be taken into account;
- issues that arise due to other interested parties;
- business impact analysis;
- risk and threat assessment;

- business continuity strategy;
- awareness programme;
- training programme;
- incident management plans;
- business continuity plans;
- business recovery plans;
- support documents such as plans, blueprints and infrastructure layouts;
- arrangements for monitoring the business continuity process;
- policy statement;
- exercise schedule and reports;
- procedures for evaluating the results of monitoring and testing;
- service-level agreements and contracts.

If the organization intends to obtain certification to ISO 22301 then the documentation must contain everything that the Standard requires.

This documentation will evolve through the life of the project and may be subject to update and amendments as the business risks and functions change. These documents therefore need to be managed securely.

Some of this documentation, such as contracts and service-level agreements, will not be created within this project but will already exist elsewhere in the organization. Copies of them, along with things like wiring diagrams and other blueprints, will be needed as part of the continuity plans so that they can be used to effect or measure a recovery. Where copies are retained, there should also be a process to ensure that they are always the *latest* copies.

There are, however, three important reasons for retaining these documents within the project:

- to provide guidance and direction in the event that recovery processes need to be instituted;
- to provide a series of processes and steps to ensure that the business continuity programme is maintained in a usable and up-to-date state;
- to provide an audit trail demonstrating what decisions were made and the information and circumstances pertaining at the time that justified those decisions.

The documentation is of vital importance to any recovery process and therefore should be protected by having a copy securely stored off site. Electronically created documents should additionally be protected under any backup and recovery procedures the organization might have in place specifically for such material.

Confidentiality needs to be applied as appropriate, as some of these documents will contain more information about the organization than it would normally provide and this may pave the way for attacks, disruption or business compromise by unauthorized users, malicious activists or rivals.

Key documents that impinge upon actual continuity and recovery situations should be immediately available to the recovery teams to facilitate their recovery processes. This means that they must be located at every key office and that those responsible for making continuity decisions must know where they are and be able to access them quickly.

All documentation should be kept as up to date as possible with versioning history and version control in place to ensure that only the latest copies are available to those responsible for using them.

Older versions may be stored for archival purposes, but they must not be confused with the live versions. A process for ensuring this needs to be developed, established and tested. Internal audit would certainly review this process.

Audit view

Any audit review will naturally use the documentation generated by the project team as part of its material for testing and confirmation. Internal audit therefore needs to undertake a thorough review of the documentation, including all the processes that surround them to ensure that documents have been prepared properly and encompass all the information provided and reflect the views of business functions.

The management of the documentation also needs to be considered to ensure that the documents themselves, as well as the organization, are not put at risk. Such issues might arise if sensitive data is included in documents given wide circulation. Any review should also cover both the ease of use of the documents and the processes for updating them.

The main stages in document management are discussed in Appendix 5.

Apart from the documents created within the project, audit will also need to reassure itself that the process of sourcing documents from other locations (e.g. contracts) is robust. This is to ensure that all such documents, whenever implemented or updated, are made available to the continuity team for incorporation into the continuity plans as appropriate.

Management review

Top management needs to undertake a review of the organization's BCMS at planned intervals to ensure its continuing suitability, adequacy and effectiveness. This review needs to take into account any actions that were identified at previous management reviews and whether these have been acted upon. It also needs to look at any internal or external changes that are relevant and that may have an impact, as well as the performance of the existing system.

Where nonconformities or problems have arisen, these should be identified and quantified. This process should include identifying corrective actions and whether there are any trends apparent. Audit reports should be taken into account in this process.

From this, top management should identify any actions for implementation or carry forward any opportunities for continual improvement.

Audit view

Internal audit should be encouraging top management to undertake such reviews and to take a serious interest in the findings and solutions. To help achieve this, audit should recommend to top management that they include business continuity as an agenda item at regular intervals but no less than every six months. This will maintain the focus and awareness.

Where top management picks up a failure to meet the requirements (a nonconformity) with the BCMS or problems with the business continuity process, audit should seek to include that aspect in their annual audit programme where possible. They can then review the circumstances of the issue and ensure corrective action is or has been taken.

4

Understanding the organization and its continuity requirements

Setting the scene

Having developed the management programme to provide a framework for its business continuity aspirations, the organization now needs to understand what exactly its assets and liabilities are. This chapter discusses undertaking and collating these assets as well as looking at the risks that bring in the liabilities and the impacts.

References

ISO 22301, clauses 6.2, 8.2.1, 8.2.2, 8.2.3.

PDCA model

This chapter forms part of the Plan (establish) phase of the business continuity life cycle.

Establish business continuity policy, objectives, targets, controls, processes and procedures relevant to improving business continuity in order to deliver results that align with the organization's overall policies and objectives.

Introduction

This is a key part of the process in that it provides an organization with an opportunity to understand what assets it holds. Equally it also provides an opportunity to assess the risks involved in holding these assets.

Organizations should be aware that some of these risks arise simply because of the assets rather than any other reason. A classic example is an online presence (or website). Simply by being there it will attract attackers. If the organization is involved in particular activities then there will be more attackers. Such activities may include financial activity, where a successful attack could lead to gain; or perhaps animal testing or government, where the attack could generate a protest or good publicity. Even perceived low-risk organizations can suffer, as they may be attacked to provide a foothold for further attacks on other locations or as a place to store material. This is sometimes known as a firebase.

Consider the not-for-profit organization that started building a web server on Friday. It had no security on it when it was left for the weekend. On Monday it was found to be full of pornography and attack software.

There are, however, plenty of risks that organizations face dependent on the nature of their business, the legal and regulatory framework they work in, their location, the surrounding geography and, not least, the risk caused by other organizations around them. Identifying and understanding these risks and the impacts they might have is the important part of understanding what could go wrong and what is needed to effect a successful recovery.

Organizational objectives

The business continuity objectives provided by top management need to:

- be consistent with the business continuity policy;
- take account of the minimum level of products and services that is acceptable to the organization to achieve its objectives;
- be measurable;
- take into account applicable requirements;
- be monitored and updated as appropriate.

The brief provided by top management for the project will show the organization's objectives simply by highlighting the parts of the business for which management most wants a continuity plan. It is, however, uncertain that this brief will be detailed enough for the project to use as its only input.

The project team will therefore have to interview key managers to determine their view of the organizational objectives. The input from these will then need to be balanced against published material such as annual accounts, policy statements and others to arrive at a view of the actual and stated directions and intentions of the organization.

It is probably a wise move to obtain top management's commitment to this statement of objectives before the project progresses too far.

In order to properly understand the nature and scope of the organization the project team needs to identify certain key functions and functionalities and document them. Table 3 illustrates the capture approaches, which are discussed later.

Table 3 Capture approaches for organizational information

Key aspects	Capture approach
How an incident will affect each of the activities of the organization and how this impact will change over time	Business impact analysis
What resources, facilities and services (both internal and external) each activity will require to commence recovery	Continuity recovery requirements analysis
An estimation of the likelihood and impact on specific activities from known threats	Risk assessment

Audit view

This statement of objectives is a key document and will provide a cornerstone of the business continuity strategy, as it will focus the project's approaches on the priority of recovery, the speed of recovery and the resources required for recovery. Internal audit should therefore review this document and the assumptions built into it.

Top management sign off should be anticipated and audit should query where this has not been achieved.

Business impact analysis

The business impact analysis is the key document in understanding the various business functions. One should be prepared for each function to identify the assets, systems and processes involved as well as the threats and risks that could eventuate. Mapped against this should be the timescale of the various recovery and continuity exercises that have to be undertaken for each business activity. It can also allow for any relationships that there might be between activities.

It achieves this by:

- documenting the impacts over time resulting from an incident causing loss or damage to a business activity;
- enabling a maximum tolerable period of disruption to be defined for each business activity;
- defining the ideal recovery time objective for each business activity;
- identifying the internal and external dependencies of each activity.

To populate the business impact analysis, the project team must develop realistic disruption options and discuss these with the various business units and functions to determine their views on the likely impacts that could result and the likely recovery time frames, needs and priorities. They should also be alert to impacts and risks that the business team may be concerned about.

The business impact analysis should consider the impact of disruption for predefined periods of time, such as one day, two days, five days and one month. Impact can take many forms, including financial loss, replacement costs, reductions in demand, financial penalties from regulatory bodies, compensation payments, loss of market reputation, loss of key staff and loss of productivity. All should be fully explored during the interviews with the various business functions, along with any other particular impacts or effects that need to be taken into account.

The outcome of the analysis and comparison of business activities and impacts will identify which areas of the business must be recovered in what sequence, how fast this process should be, and what resources are required at each stage.

The business impact analysis forms part of the business continuity management system (BCMS) documentation and it should be the responsibility of one function to keep it as up to date as possible. The latest copies of the business impact analysis should be identified to ensure that only these live copies are used in any determination or assessment of recovery options and processes. Although the project team will probably prepare the first business impact analysis, its subsequent management and update may become the responsibility of the particular business function involved.

It follows that a properly researched and prepared business impact analysis would allow management to predict the likely scale of disruption and impact on business activities in advance of major business changes such as a relocation or introduction of a new supply chain. This means that these documents can be used for measuring existing systems as well as previewing planned ones.

Audit view

It is important that the various business impact analysis documents reflect as objective a view of the real impacts and recovery needs of the key business activities as is possible. Subjective assessments should be held to the minimum, as they will depend on the outlook of the interviewee or the analyst rather than the facts.

For some events computer modelling may be necessary. In the case of weather or geological factors this may be the only easy solution. In many cases, however, there will be experience of what has happened before, both within the organization and beyond. Where possible such experience needs to be supported by documentary evidence.

The information contained in the business impact analysis will be very important for anyone attempting to compromise or attack the organization, as it will show the business's weaknesses and how they are to be tackled. Clearly therefore these documents must have limited circulation and need to be protected. Internal audit should therefore include a security assessment or review of the way these documents are protected, stored, transmitted, destroyed and managed.

The business impact analysis development process is long and complex but it is a key step in identifying issues that the organization may face. It is therefore a process that audit should encourage. Internal audit should also reinforce the project team in seeking to ensure that business functions make preparation and updating of the business impact analyses part of the ongoing process to capture information about new systems and changes to old ones. By this approach the continuity plans can continue to evolve as the organization does.

Continuity recovery requirements analysis

While the business impact analysis is the primary medium for gathering the raw data and establishing how business activities can recover and in what timescale, a continuity requirements analysis may be used to provide the information that enables the scale of the appropriate continuity measures to be determined.

It achieves this through the collection and collation of the numbers and types of resources needed to resume and continue business activities at an appropriate level to satisfy management requirements, and any external obligations. This will then demonstrate the scale of the measures required for effective recovery.

This information collection and analysis is usually undertaken at the same time as the business impact analysis.

Once collected, the information feeds directly into the business continuity strategy stage (Chapter 5). At that point, the resource requirements for recovering each activity can be used to evaluate and calculate the cost of alternative recovery options.

Audit view

This is a key process in understanding the nature of the organization and its business activities, as it enables the depth of resources required for recovery to be estimated. Internal audit should therefore closely review the figures and assumptions to ensure that the project team has made reasonable and justifiable assumptions. If the assessments are not accurate then actual recovery of the business activity, if ever required, may not happen.

Key steps for audit in its review of these documents will be to ensure that the project team has:

- obtained sign off by the owner (or other responsible person) of the various business activities to confirm the accuracy of information supplied;
- received the support of the senior manager or sponsor responsible for the business continuity programme for the conclusions reached;
- checked with senior management whether there are any proposed business changes or other considerations that may affect the findings and conclusions reached.

Internal audit may still wish to re-perform some of the calculations and analyses to confirm that consistent logic and decisions are used throughout, and that the margin for error and approximation is sufficiently low to ensure proper decisions have been made.

Useful audit scopes for reviewing this part of the process include:

- reviewing the process for the business impact analysis undertaken and consulting with the business to establish if their requirements had been appropriately captured;
- determining the adequacy and effectiveness of the identification of impacts resulting from disruptions and incident scenarios that can affect the organization and the techniques used to quantify and qualify such impacts.

The scope should also include the establishment of critical processes, their recovery priorities and interdependencies in order that recovery time and recovery point objectives are understood.

The recovery point objective is the point in time to which work should be restored following a service disruption. Essentially this means the latest time that the work could be trusted. For most organizations this is a trade-off between the cost of sophisticated and expensive backup systems against the risk of losing, or having to re-enter, some data or information.

Statutory duties

Each organization is bound by a range of legislation that defines many obligations and responsibilities. These will be dependent upon the needs of the country and business sectors concerned but may include some or all of the following:

- data protection;
- human rights;
- disabilities;
- health and safety;
- discrimination;
- taxation.

In addition there will be many other legal and regulatory issues, some of which will be country or sector-specific or relate to particular trades such as exports and armaments trading.

The project team must seek to understand all the legal obligations that are in place and with which the organization must comply. Given the weight of legislation in place from international, national and local governments, it may be that this task is outsourced to the organization's legal advisers.

A view needs to be taken on how this legislation affects the organization and in particular any obligations that it must fulfil.

Details of these obligations need to be built into the parameters document defining the organization's obligations during and after recovery.

Audit view

Again, internal audit needs to assure itself that this list of obligations is both full and accurate. This may mean reviewing the source material or conducting discussions with legal experts to confirm that at least key legislation has been covered.

While the role of audit here is to check the findings, it should not just be re-performing the work, as that would be counterproductive. It needs to use best endeavours and reasonable effort to assure itself that the project team has undertaken appropriate due diligence and that its findings are going to safeguard the organization and not create any new or unnecessary risks.

Operating environment

The project team needs to review the way the organization operates across all its business functions to determine what it actually needs in place to enable it to operate.

If, for example, a business function is heavily dependent on a resource or facility then the project team should look at the options that exist to replace or supplement that aspect in the event that an incident should close that particular option.

Cost may not be a determining factor if the business is going to keep going, but cost increases will hit the bottom line and ongoing high cost may jeopardize that particular business function.

The aim therefore is to review what constraints currently exist, determine how much of a threat those risks pose and whether there are any mitigating actions. Once this is known then the plan can factor in these options. The relevant business functions need to be involved in this process as, apart from cost and convenience, quality and contractual terms may be an issue. The business function would be aware of how the options stack up against the one they are currently using.

Audit view

Internal audit should perform routine testing to determine if the appropriate actions have been taken to identify the key parameters of the operating environment.

As this aspect does have significant operational impact it would be as well for audit to sample some of the business functions and ensure that their views are being properly represented and that the constraints and opportunities of the existing operational environment are correctly reflected in the business continuity model.

As with the other aspects looked at, there needs to be a process to continue to monitor and capture any changes in the operational environment that might impact upon assumptions in the plan or the plan itself.

Identifying activities, assets and resources

This is probably one of the largest and longest parts of the process. It ideally requires the project team to visit every function within the organization and every company outside the organization that supports any function or business service within the organization.

The purpose is to capture data and information on all the assets held and the way they are used. This information will then be used to determine an appropriate recovery strategy and to highlight any resource dependencies.

The assets will fall into the following categories:

- people;
- premises;
- technology;
- information;
- supplies;
- stakeholders.

Before attempting this task, the project team should have devised some form of documentation to capture the information in a standard way. Failure to do this will mean that data captured in one function may not be compatible with that collected elsewhere.

Internal audit will have built up a collection of data and information on many of the organization's assets and should be involved in helping the project team to build lists of what is in use. Other key players for providing information will include human resources, IT and any central repositories for contracts. Beyond this, many of the links and interdependencies will only become obvious and visible when interviewing the various business and operational functions.

Once the data has been collected it can be analysed for use in developing the business continuity plan.

Audit view

Although audit should be a willing player in this project and provide the information requested, it should still be aware that as part of its assurance role it needs to vet the information that the project team are using. This means that it should assess the material it provided in the same way as that provided by others to ensure it is valid and up to date.

This exercise may provide internal audit with some information and links or interdependencies that it was not aware of. Although these can be verified during a review of this project, further investigation would require a separate audit exercise.

People

In essence the requirement is to capture information about the people who are involved in meeting the organizational objectives. This should include every employee and many others who, although outside the organization, contribute to its objectives by virtue of the work they do.

This is usually achieved by visiting every function in the organization and its extended environment to ascertain:

- the number and type of staff posts;
- which posts are essential and when;

- the type of work undertaken;
- how this contributes to the business objectives;
- the importance of this work in meeting the business objectives;
- the interdependencies this work has with others;
- identifying how these interdependencies work;
- the needs of these people, from stationery to information flows;
- the management and reporting lines;
- any succession plans for key posts;
- any arrangements in place for contacting all staff in the event of an incident.

This information should also capture any constraints on the staff or the work they undertake. This might include disabled staff with special access, equipment, working or other needs. It might also include 'hot-desking' where staff have no specific desk in an office but use whichever desks or cubicles that are vacant when they arrive.

Another category of staff is those that work off site. These could be contractors to other organizations, mobile staff such as sales representatives and those who work from home or other remote locations. Their needs and dependencies need to be recognized, and it should be ensured that they are fully involved with this information capture process.

For all staff that travel regularly on organizational business there should be an appreciation of the mode used. Each main form of transport (bicycle, bus, train, car and plane) can bring benefits and risks and if they are being regularly used for business then these need to be understood. The review should also understand whether staff and managers regularly travel together or separately, as this may have an impact upon the risks involved. Some organizations, for example, ban executives from travelling together to reduce the risks of one incident affecting them all.

Consider the financial organization with two head offices located many kilometres apart. Staff and executives regularly travel between the two offices. The primary travel option is by air, meaning that many staff and executives are travelling in the same aircraft.

Consider also that a number of organizations have banned teams, branch offices and other self-contained units from buying lottery tickets together. This is to reduce the risk that if they win they will all quit together.

Table 4 includes a selection of the questions that need to be addressed in this data capture process.

Table 4 Personnel resources data capture questions

Issue	Yes	No	Don't know
Is staff personal information on file, such as staff contact details? (Including for temporary and contract workers?)			
Is an up-to-date and accessible copy of this information stored off site?			
Are there members of staff with first aid training?			
Do you check references fully?			
Do you have an up-to-date job description and hierarchy chart for each business function? (Including for temporary and contract workers?)			
Does each business function have a staff succession plan in place?			
Can essential staff that may be injured or unavailable be replaced by other staff?			

Audit view

Clearly a standard range of matters will need to be covered in the process of determining staffing issues. However, there may be aspects that are unique to each organization and these should also be covered. Internal audit should be mindful of these issues when reviewing the documentation and be prepared to challenge the project team on any uncertain or unclear aspects.

Audit should also be aware that in certain circumstances an organization or function may require additional staff to handle enquiries and problems in the immediate aftermath of an incident. This aspect may or may not be anticipated by the functions involved, but audit should be aware of the potential needs and ensure that such considerations are built into the plans.

Premises

While the basic purpose of this part of the exercise is to capture significant information about the offices, warehouses, store areas and other buildings owned or used by the organization, this may form only part of the exercise.

The opportunity may also be taken to investigate the wider geography of the premises with a view to determining more information. This work could involve looking at:

- infrastructure connections, including utilities, communications and transport arrangements;
- topography and soil composition;
- location of emergency services;
- local facilities such as hospitals, schools and nursing homes;
- unique, historic or other cultural resources;
- hazardous materials, including production, storage and transport depots;
- property characteristics such as construction type;
- hot spots – features such as sites where significant amounts of dangerous goods are stored or transported;
- high-risk areas such as rivers or scrubland that regularly catches fire;
- vulnerable infrastructure such as petrol stations, airports and military facilities;
- potential terrorist targets;
- local population size and distribution;
- whether any warning systems exist and their features.

Although not every organization will want all this level of detail, some of it, particularly that relating to the risks that may be caused by neighbouring organizations, is vitally important and needs to be collected for each office involved.

Where the organization has mobile and remote workers it may be necessary to include any premises that these workers use, including their own homes, in the review. A similar process may need to be taken for any outsourced functions.

Table 5 shows some of the issues that could be covered while gathering data about each building and business location.

Table 5 Premises and location data capture questions

Issue	Yes	No	Don't know
Are there emergency evacuation procedures for the location (e.g. in the event of fire or bombing)?			
Are the emergency exits clearly marked?			
Are emergency drills practised regularly?			
Are there primary and secondary evacuation assembly points?			
Is a floor plan to the location or building available?			
Is the building accessible at all times?			
Are fire safety procedures in place?			
Are water sprinklers fitted?			
Do computer rooms have fire protection systems, (e.g. water, gas, dry powder) for fire retardation?			
Is there an appropriate and regularly maintained security alarm system?			
Is advice or training on security given to relevant staff?			
Are contractors checked fully (i.e. the company as well as each individual)?			
Where fitted, are external fences and doors regularly checked?			
Are end-of-day inspections carried out to confirm staff have left and the premises are secure?			
Is there access to an alternative workspace to use in an incident?			
Does anyone in the business function know the location and operation of the mains switches and valves (e.g. for electricity, gas and water)?			
Are services regularly checked for correct operation (e.g. plumbing, heating and air conditioning)?			
Are electrical devices checked regularly?			

Audit view

The information collected in this phase of the project could have significant value to the organization in respect of security as well as business continuity. It may expose issues that elevate the security risk of one or more premises used by the organization. Audit should be aware of the additional value of this and any information collected during the project and ensure that the knowledge is not lost or simply left in the project but is used to the overall benefit of the organization. Some of the geological data if collected may, for example, highlight risks that have been unappreciated until now.

If the data generated is sensitive in this way then audit also needs to ensure that it is, and remains, adequately protected and safeguarded.

Once the data is captured for all locations then it needs to be cross-referenced to the various functions that use those sites to build a profile of the organization and its distribution.

Technology

Most organizations use a wide range of technology to perform their business. This can range from calculators through computers to complete production lines.

This potentially wide range of technological needs and solutions means that the project team must collect a broad range of information on where this equipment is, what it is used for and its relevance to business services and functions.

Large items of equipment will have been purchased through a capital budget and will almost certainly be recorded in the organization's asset register. However, with the increasing miniaturization of equipment and the price falls in the marketplace, a lot of the supporting technology may be below the threshold for inclusion in an asset register. If that is the case then some effort may need to be made to capture this information in another way. The IT department will, no doubt, be monitoring the assets under its wing for both security and connectivity and therefore should hold records of equipment that could be useful.

The processes to manage computer hardware are likely to show when items were purchased, what configuration they are and where they are located. Clearly, the larger the organization, the more complex their records will be, as they will need to manage thousands of machines potentially in multiple local and overseas locations.

Similarly there should be software management processes in place to ensure that only legal and licensed software is in use. These software management programs may also provide some useful information on what software is in use and by whom.

Software records can be correlated with staff and business functional information to cross-check what software is used by the different business processes and where else similar products are in use.

Many software auditing programs will also detect information about the hardware they are running on, and accordingly can be used as part of the hardware audit solution.

Purchase contracts may identify the type of equipment in use as well as any constraints that the organization may be under in using or maintaining such equipment.

Other equipment and technology may only be identified as part of the business function data-gathering exercise when considering business process dependencies.

Table 6 illustrates some of the questions that could be posed during the technology data-gathering exercise.

Table 6 Technology data capture questions

Issue	Yes	No	Don't know
Have the critical IT systems for each business function been identified?			
Is a documented and tested IT disaster recovery plan already in place?			
Are the relevant staff aware of any IT disaster recovery plan that may be in place?			
Have any IT recovery times been determined?			
Are documented IT security policies and procedures in place?			

Issue	Yes	No	Don't know
Are all staff aware of IT security policies and procedures?			
Has key equipment been identified?			
Is an inventory of equipment kept and maintained?			
Are there controls over the movements of business or organizational equipment?			
Is vital computer information stored off site?			

Audit view

This is a very large area and may require the setting up of sub-projects to capture this information alongside the main project. This would reduce the lead time for collecting all the data, but would require the sub-project teams to liaise closely to ensure that equipment needs were properly linked to functional requirements.

Internal audit would need to undertake some work to ensure the validity of the findings but given the scale of this aspect, re-performing large-scale verifications would not be cost-effective.

Audit should therefore concentrate on the larger capital items and ensure that items in the selected sample should all be linked to a location, a business function and a business owner. It is, however, often the case with computer software that the business owner is not necessarily the user. In these circumstances, the owner gives permission for the user to access or use the software. It is the security function or IT department that then enables this access.

Backup arrangements

Backup copies of essential business information and software should be created regularly and adequate backup facilities should be provided to ensure that all essential business information and software could be recovered following an incident or media failure.

Backup arrangements for individual systems should be regularly tested to ensure they meet the requirements of the organization for its recovery needs.

The following guidelines should be considered.

- A minimum level of backup information, together with accurate and complete records of the backup copies and documented restoration procedures, should be stored in a remote location, at a sufficient distance to escape any damage from an incident at the main site.
- At least three generations or cycles of backup information should be retained for important business applications.
- Backup information should be given an appropriate level of physical and environmental protection consistent with the standards applied at the main site. The controls applied to media at the main site should be extended to cover the backup site.
- Backup media should be regularly tested, where practicable, to ensure that they can be relied upon for recovery use when necessary.
- Restoration procedures should be regularly checked and tested to ensure they are effective and can be completed within the time allotted in the operational procedures for recovery.
- The retention period for essential business information, and also any requirement for archive copies to be permanently retained, should be determined. This may be covered in local legislation or guidance.

Generations of backup data are important as it enables recovery to be achieved quickly and easily. A typical backup structure for a small organization working a 5-day week may be as follows.

- Monday to Thursday – back up each night the data that has changed during the day. Store the backup media off site. This media is recycled weekly with the Monday one (for example) being returned the following Monday to be overwritten by that night's backup data.
- Friday – a full backup of the system and all data. This backup would be kept off site for a month before reuse.
- Monthly – at the end of each month a full backup would be taken. These backups would be stored off site for 12 months.
- Annually – at the end of each year a full backup would be taken. This backup would be stored indefinitely.

By this process, the organization can use a combination of annual, monthly, weekly and daily backup media to restore the system depending on the severity of the incident. Only changes made, or data added, after the last backup would then need to be re-input.

Many organizations, however, use real-time systems where the rate of data change is faster than can be safely accommodated by using an end-of-day backup arrangement. Such business functions might include trading floors and similar environments. In these cases the file servers are set up to write saved data twice – each time to a different hard disk. This means that in the event of a failure happening to a disk drive the problem can be overcome without interrupting the workflow. There is, however, no reason why this second data write has to be to a hard disk on the same machine. It could be to a remote machine. This latter process is sometimes known as electronic vaulting. It resolves the issue of the incident happening, not just to a disk drive, but also to the entire room or building.

Backup processes for mainframes and network-based servers are normally well established, with the organization taking full responsibility for all aspects. For desktop-based systems, however, employees will require clear guidance on what material is covered in the organization's automated backup systems and what backup is the responsibility of individuals or departments.

In some organizations, users of networked machines can choose to have their machines backed up simply by leaving them switched on and connected to the network. However, if users switch them off then no backup is taken. Other organizations simply take no responsibility for data stored on local hard drives and make no effort to back them up. In these cases, the users become responsible for storing valuable data on the servers, backing it up themselves, or risking its loss.

In distributed data and distributed processing environments it becomes very important for the organization's policies and procedures to clearly define roles and responsibilities for both providing and ensuring adequate backup of data.

Organizational backup files may be too large to allow individual files to be recovered from them should a user experience difficulties. If this is likely to be the case, users must be alerted to the fact so they can decide whether to take responsibility for holding a spare copy.

If users are given a part to play in storing backups, they should be given clear guidance on how to store such media to ensure that heat, magnetism or other actions or agents do not damage them. Organizations should also consider the potential security problems and issues of users connecting their own portables (including handhelds, USB flash drives or other media) to organizational machines in order to take backup copies.

Similarly there should be guidelines on the use of removable storage devices and removable media that could, or does, carry organizational data or backups. This is particularly true if these devices are to be connected to, or used, off site and/or on non-organizational machines.

Backup copies should be stored off site so that they do not suffer from the same incident that may hit the organization itself. This is especially true if the incident is at neighbouring premises but results in access to the organization's premises being prevented, or in the case of wide area incidents or disruptions affecting electrical power, communications, transportation, water or other critical services.

Backup media should be recycled regularly to ensure that they continue to work properly.

Audit view

There is an important balance to be struck between the needs of the organization in ensuring that there are sufficient backups of its data and the security of the organization in allowing staff to take backups off site.

In most organizations the desktop machines are deemed to be only for processing. All organizational data must be stored on central servers or mainframes to be covered by the regular backup processes. Any data stored locally is therefore deemed to be 'personal' and is outside the scope of the formal backup processes.

Although this solves the bigger issue it still leaves data, which may or may not be 'personal', on a local machine and thus available for downloading. Audit needs to consider this whole issue as a separate review and determine what processes should be in place and how necessary safeguards should be implemented and enforced.

Backup routines should be examined to ensure that they do provide the level of secure backup needed for recovery. Audit should also look at sampling the backup media to ensure not only that it is usable but also that full recovery can be achieved from it.

Where electronic vaulting is in place, audit needs to ensure that the recovery procedures can actually bring the backup data back online immediately. The further the original data site is from the backup location, the longer the time lag is in the second writing. Consequently, if the backup data centre is too far away, there may be an appreciable time difference between the original and backup data being written. In a highly intensive situation, this time difference, although it may be microseconds, may result in data being lost if the original system is switched out and the backup system takes over.

Some ideas for audit scopes to review this aspect include:

- reviewing backup material to ensure that it is current and documented appropriately;
- ensuring that critical systems and data are adequately and frequently backed up to protect the business operations and integrity of the organization;
- ensuring that full recovery can be achieved;
- ensuring that backup data remains in a usable and accessible form;
- ensuring that data storage facilities provide the appropriate environmental conditions to prevent deterioration or damage to media;
- evaluating recovery and backup plans;
- evaluating any off-site storage facilities, especially with respect to their security and their environmental footprint.

Information

Establishing the location of information is probably the hardest of all the tasks, as it can exist in a wide range of forms in myriad places from computer systems through paper records to people's minds.

Managing this data and information mix has become considerably easier with the release of software that can detect patterns in various types of unstructured data (such as electronic mails, faxes, voice and video). This software can allow such data to be pulled together and categorized for storage and use within the organization. However, this software is expensive and may not be an option for many organizations.

Tacit information that moves between people can only be captured if recorded or turned into another form (such as video). However, this is a major source of information flow within organizations and contributes much to how organizations are run. It may therefore be necessary to take steps to capture this expertise.

Many financial institutions and others have already used this approach to build 'expert systems'. These are computer programs that follow the 'rules' used by human experts to make decisions. Where these decisions would normally be of the 'yes' or 'no' variety there are no problems, but when it is necessary to build in the ability for the program to make subjective decisions then a 'neural network' is required. This enables the program to learn from past decisions and so each new decision is honed on the basis of experience. The technicalities of these systems are beyond the scope of this book but for those organizations with a need for this sort of information usage, these could be an option.

These approaches can thus help an organization to formalize and capture the information that it may need in order to recover properly, especially if the incident being recovered from is the loss of key staff.

From these records the project team will be able to ascertain which computers process key organizational data and where computer-based and paper-based records are stored.

The security and backup arrangements for this information also needs to be collated, as this can have an effect on how the data can be accessed and whether those doing so need special access permissions or protocols.

Some organizations use enterprise resource planning systems to provide centralized systems that all staff access, or databases to hold the bulk of their customer and business data. In these cases, the project teams need to be particularly aware of these and how they are managed. Issues like location, protection, access control, backup and recovery are key to these systems as they will be at the heart of the organization and its business services and offerings.

Table 7 highlights some of the points that need to be covered during the information data-gathering exercise.

Audit view

Internal audit may have undertaken an information audit as part of its regular audit plan. Such reviews are becoming more common as the need to manage and secure organizational information rises up the agenda. This importance is being driven by threats to personal data and the opportunities for data mining that make better use of stored and available data to improve business services and offerings.

Table 7 Information data capture questions

Issue	Yes	No	Don't know
Is vital computer information stored off site?			
Is information regularly backed up?			
Are critical documents adequately protected?			
Are copies of critical records stored at a separate location?			
Are critical documents stored in a suitable environment so they will not deteriorate?			

If there is an information audit available it should be provided to the project team with appropriate safeguards. These will assure that only the collected data is made available and not any projections or extrapolations. It should also reflect any security issues and not provide personal or other sensitive information that has been derived or added by the audit team.

Audit should also be mindful that a lot of organizations hold data on databases. Security within databases is essentially managed through 'views', which enable users in different parts of the organization to see only what they need to see to perform their jobs. Nothing that the project team does should be allowed to compromise this job segregation or make organizational data available to unauthorized users.

An additional aspect is the data that the project team itself generates. This clearly needs to be protected such that only team members (and perhaps even only a few of those) are allowed to make changes to any data captured. Access controls can be instituted to permit users any combination of the following options:

- read;
- write;
- delete.

This granularity of access control enables restrictions to be placed on users to ensure that only those with the appropriate authority can perform certain tasks.

It may even be necessary to restrict matters further so that only designated computers or printers may be used for processing and printing business continuity material. This would not be normal but is available as an option if required.

Supplies

All organizations are dependent on some form of supplies: from utility services, through business support services to raw and part-finished materials. The project team needs to identify these supplies and factor into their processes where this service comes from, how it is delivered and when it is provided.

These supplies may also include those provided by other suppliers, such as outsourced services or subcontracted work. In the case of a virtual organization there may be no materials as such, but a collection of electronic connections delivering services, support and customers.

Whatever the situation, the project team needs to capture the information and incorporate it into the matrix identifying inputs and relating these back to business functions and business services.

Table 8 highlights key questions that need to be posed to each business function and organizational support function.

Table 8 Supplier data capture questions

Issue	Yes	No	Don't know
Have key suppliers been identified?			
Do key suppliers have their own business continuity plan?			
Have alternative sources for critical supplies been identified?			
Are the up-to-date contact details for all suppliers held in a convenient form?			

Audit view

It is extremely unlikely that there are many organizations conducting business operations that do not require supplies in one form or another. However, validating the particular services received may be awkward as some will be taken for granted, such as basic utility services like heat, light and telecommunications. They may also include support from suppliers such as replacement of faulty items and help in installing or using new products, although strictly this aspect is considered as a stakeholder rather than a supply matter.

Internal audit will have reviewed some of the organizational inputs as part of earlier audits and will be aware of the more significant issues; in particular, the need to understand how often these supplies are received, whether there are any security or special arrangements that may apply and whether there are specific business requirements.

Issues that might be encountered include the following.

- 'Just-in-time' systems where goods are supplied on a predetermined and contracted basis. Failure to deliver 'just-in-time' items on time can result in penalty payments under the contract, but equally so can failure to accept deliveries.
- Virtual services that are received and offered out again, perhaps with the organization making profit on the buy or sell transaction. Here the organization is totally dependent upon the services or information being available and that the customers can (in their turn) access it. These services can be affected by other remote issues outside the direct control of the organization and its suppliers (e.g. computer viruses).
- Automatic top-up systems where computer programs issue orders based on predetermined ordering and inventory holding figures. In essence, as customers buy goods the inventory goes down. This figure is monitored and when it reaches a certain level an order is placed to buy more. The system may have made the order but delivery times may then be outside its control.
- Goods to be received have specific security, value or control issues and need to be handled in a special way. This would include, for example, bonding for tobacco and alcohol, and security restrictions for banknotes and armaments. The project team needs to be clear on these restrictions.

Audit will therefore expect to look closely at the findings in this category to ensure that the organization and its suppliers have been properly assessed.

Stakeholders

In considering the stakeholder obligations of the organization, the project team should take into account the organizational responsibilities with respect to:

- shareholders;
- employees;
- customers;
- trading partners;
- local communities;
- government;
- regulator.

Not all of these will be relevant for every organization and there may be others that will apply in specific circumstances.

The point about stakeholder responsibilities is that none of them is optional and all must coexist so there is no detriment to one while favouring another.

The project team must therefore consult with these stakeholders – or at least a reasonable sample – to gain an understanding of their expectations and concerns about how the organization could continue to serve or work with them during and after an incident.

Findings should be documented and built into the parameters for the project. The various categories of stakeholder within the organization have widely differing needs and responsibilities, so the data obtainable from them is also going to be different.

To a large extent employees will contribute as members of the organization's functional units, but they may also be shareholders or customers, or be involved in the local community or local government.

Consider the IT consultant employed by one financial organization. Every so often he would leave work early in a chauffeured limousine to perform his duties as mayor of the local borough council, where he could be involved in decisions potentially affecting his employer.

Where employees of the organization are working off site there may also be other players involved outside those supporting the organization. Employees at home for example may not have the same telecommunications provider as the organization. There may be different utilities involved. If any remote working employees are key to the business objectives then these issues need to be drawn out by the project team.

Trading partners and customers tend to have arm's-length relationships with an organization and are bound by contract, whim or by mutual need. This means that their perception of the organization and how far they would work with it in adversity could be untested waters. The project team needs to probe this aspect further. There may be contractual obligations that a trading partner has to meet (taking minimum levels of stock for example) that oblige them to find other outlets if one of their trading partners has a serious problem.

Unions will be seeking to protect their members' interests and to ensure that they are safeguarded no matter what happens to the organization. Their concerns clearly need to be recognized in staff communications, staff welfare and other matters that affect the conditions of employment.

Local communities may or may not want the organization there at all. For some it could be an opportunity for employment while for others it will be an eyesore, an accident waiting happen and a blight on the value of their houses. There is little that can be done about such negative feelings but the project team might see an opportunity for 'good neighbour' exercises as part of the overall awareness exercises that help spread the word about continuity programmes.

The government machine at all levels is looking for compliance with the law, the creation of minimum disruption and prompt payment of taxes and other dues. Any regulator involved will be looking at sectoral and other matters to ensure compliance or even to curtail activities if necessary. All of these could provide constraints on what the organization can do and how quickly it can react to a changing environment.

Finally, the emergency services, although often part of the broad government machine, need to be looked at separately. They provide support, guidance and assistance in the event of problems. They do have standardized approaches and ways of doing things, and organizations need to mesh with them rather than expecting things to be the other way round. Although they will accommodate organizational needs as far as possible they may need to dictate certain conditions. For example how quickly they can reach a site, or how far up a building ordinary or special fire appliances can reach. These constraining factors need to be recorded to ensure that they are carried through to the next phase.

Table 9 highlights two important questions that need to be posed at this stage of the process.

Table 9 Stakeholder data capture questions

Issue	Yes	No	Don't know
Are up-to-date contact details held for key stakeholders?			
Is there a mechanism for communicating with key stakeholders during an incident?			

Audit view

The range of inputs is going to be diverse but the project team should be bringing them all forward into the analysis phase.

Internal audit should review the documentation to confirm reasonableness and to ensure that it has captured the full range of stakeholder obligations. There may also be a need to carry out some follow-up discussions or spot checks with some of the stakeholders to understand if the correct weight has been given to the various obligations recorded.

Audit should also be aware that these obligations will change over time and ensure that the project has a process in place for capturing these changes and updating the base document and, if necessary, the plan to encompass the new requirements.

Audit needs also to be aware of its own role in the organization, which is to provide assurance to management. If potential problems or weaknesses with stakeholders and the arrangements they have with the organization are identified this may lead to other issues in the future and audit may need to take that into account in its future activities.

Risk assessment

The purpose of risk assessment within business continuity is to:

- aid in identifying potential causes of interruption to an organization or business activity;

- assess the probability of the interruption occurring;
- determine the impact of the interruption actually taking place.

To aid in its review of the organization and its business functions, internal audit may wish to employ a variety of risk analysis tools. Although there are a number of these, the main requirement is to look at both external and internal influences. This can be achieved using analysis frameworks. Most organizations will already have a preferred method of risk assessment but the following three options can be used appropriately in this context:

- PESTEL;
- Seven S's;
- SWOT.

These are discussed in Appendix 2 along with tables to illustrate their use.

Another approach is to use ISO 31000:2009 *Risk management — principles and guidelines*, which provides principles and generic guidelines on risk management. It can be used by any type of organization for a wide range of activities including business continuity. This Standard is also considered further in Appendix 2.

Although the approaches could be used for any part of the organization it is important to restrict the risk assessment purely to the aspects of the organization and its business activities for which a planned recovery is required, to save wasted time and effort.

Audit view

Risk assessment is an essential prerequisite to understanding issues confronting the organization. The wider the assessment, the better the understanding of the risks. However, there is a danger of going too far or being sidetracked in this. Audit should therefore be conscious of the potential for those inexperienced at working with risks to be seduced by them and delve too far and too deep when reviewing the project team's work.

Most modern internal audit functions use risk as a way of assessing and prioritizing the aspects of an organization that need review. In view of this they should be able to bring a great deal of expertise to bear on the risks facing the organization and their likely impacts and probabilities.

Evaluating key threats

This is another very large area to consider. It is not perhaps very complex; rather it is the breadth of the risks that face an organization that is potentially overwhelming. Considering which ones could disrupt business functions enough to require a continuity plan is a further refinement to a difficult problem.

It requires the project team to identify:

- the key business activities;
- the actions that support these activities;
- what would happen if any of these activities were disrupted;
- if and how the impact of a disruption might change over time;
- how long the organization could continue to operate without that activity;
- what level of the activity is required on recovery;
- how long before normal service needs to be resumed.

It is perhaps well to consider risks as coming from certain directions, possibly as a starting point:

- static threats that surround the organization;
- operational threats that affect the business services;
- pandemics;
- regulatory threats;
- terrorist and cyber threats;
- weather and environment;
- internal threats;
- transitory threats.

It also has to be acknowledged that every threat is also an opportunity. A risk to a business function, for example, creates an opportunity that could be exploited by the business. One example is advertising. Organizations whose businesses include newspapers are seeing advertising moving towards internet-based media. To the newspaper business this is a threat requiring a continuity plan. However, to the internet-based companies this is an opportunity worth building a business around.

Breaking risks and threats into the above categories tends to make them more manageable and easier to understand and deal with.

Static threats

These are the fixed threats from having premises in the particular location.

They will include the building itself, which may have particular constructional features that make it susceptible to damage, such as a flat roof that leaks or perhaps might contain dangerous levels of asbestos. Similarly, the location may bring problems like potential floods, subsidence or toxic fumes.

Equally, the purpose of the building may create potential risks. In this context a building that processes valuable or confidential material will have additional security to protect it. If any of this is penetrated, or fails, then the threats have increased. The access points, roof, walls and underground services may all need reviewing for potential weaknesses. Dependence on one utility company may also be perceived to be a threat.

The area around the building may hold significant risks, including main roads, railways, overflying aircraft and a nearby water supply or river. A local petrol station may be an issue, as would be a high-profile terrorist target or an organization providing high-risk services or items and therefore potentially subject to criminal attack.

Operational threats affecting business services

In this category should come those threats and risks that are directly related to running the business service. These include creation, production, storage and distribution.

Different business services will have different requirements, dependencies and needs. A manufacturing line, for example, will require raw materials to come in and will produce items that may be finished items or themselves become raw materials for another production line. The incoming and outgoing items may need special handling and storage, as with food or chemicals for example, or they may require large warehouses or ground space for storage.

Service industries usually require customers to access their premises and offer services in accordance with customers' expectations, such as hotel rooms, fashion accessories or airline flights. They will, however, need efficient back offices and systems to enable them to manage their stock, services and materials and to bill customers accordingly. They may also need processes in place to manage the effects of increasing social media usage, as adverse comments about services – whether true or false – can be spread very quickly and very widely.

Virtual organizations on the other hand will probably require only reliable and efficient computer-based storage, robust software and very good communications lines to ensure that they remain in business.

Pandemics

While most organizations can cope with the fluctuating staff numbers due to holidays and sickness, there is a high risk that organizations would be unable to cope with an epidemic or pandemic that reduced their staff numbers significantly. Perhaps even more troubling would be an illness that was transmitted and retransmitted through the workforce such that the epidemic effects went on for a long time.

Any form of epidemic or pandemic might bring disruption with it if the survival rates were high but if they were low then there would not just be short-term loss of staff and knowledge, but long-term effects as well.

In both cases, small organizations are likely to fare worse as they generally have the minimum staff numbers they need and would not have the surplus capacity that most large organizations have.

Regulatory threats

There is a wide range of legislation and regulation surrounding all organizations whatever their sector and location. Much of this regulation is found across every jurisdiction such as taxation, data protection, and health and safety. There is, however, a great complexity in detail and in the way regulation can be applied in different places.

The burden of legislation is increasing year by year and there is an onus on organizations to remain aware of all the issues that could affect them. Legislation may be retrospective or may introduce one-off or short-term effects and these can represent serious potential threats for those not monitoring the situation.

Terrorist and cyber threats

There has been a growing risk from terrorist and cyber threats for some years. To a large extent this is due to the rise in the value of information (including money) that is held electronically and the awareness that computer-based systems can be taken over and controlled remotely.

A wide variety of people from those acting on their own and out to prove themselves, right through to government-sponsored attack teams are active in the field. There are a wealth of reasons for this: some may be trying to penetrate other computer systems for malicious purposes, some are disseminating viruses and other malicious software while others have commercial interests at heart. Whatever the reason, for an organization subject to electronic attack, the results can be devastating.

Intrusion and detection monitoring software and systems are part of the solution as these will at least enable the organization to understand that it is under attack. Unfortunately, it is all too easy for an attack to take place but the realization of its occurrence to follow sometime after, when valued commercial information is already in the public domain or employee data is being offered for sale.

Weather and environment

With the widely anticipated changes in climate due to global warming there is an increasing threat to organizations from changing and unusual weather patterns. Such effects will not only cover storms, rain, wind and so on, but will have further reaching consequences. These could include effects on food supplies and drinking water.

Other issues include attempts to reduce reliance on fossil fuels, which may change the way activities happen, and the impacts of controls, cartels, local protectionism and foreign governments on the supplies of commodities.

Organizations demonstrating greater green credentials may steal business from those that do not react to the changes as quickly.

Internal threats

One of the often underrated but statistically important aspects is the role of staff in bringing threats into the organization. There are two primary reasons for this, with the first being accidental and the second being deliberate.

Accidental problems occur when staff perform tasks outside their competence or training. They can also occur as accidents plain and simple.

Consider the experienced IT employee who thought he knew how to add an additional disk drive to a system to provide extra backup storage. The installation did not simply fail, it bought down the entire network and the backup system for three days.

Other problems are deliberate, where staff and other users try to bring down systems. Computer hackers do not have to come from outside the organization but may start their activities inside. Often deliberate actions result from low staff morale or disaffected staff but some people do take jobs specifically to gain access to an organization with the intention of causing disruption and/or gaining information.

Transitory threats

As the name implies these are threats that exist for a short period of time and then pass. They will include a range of events that would not perhaps appear on the normal risk radar, such as:

- a march, protest or political rally;
- a temporary traffic diversion or disruption;
- a bomb threat at a neighbouring organization.

Organizations therefore need to be aware of what is happening in their local environment and consider how such events might affect them. A pessimistic view might best be adopted for this purpose.

Audit view

Evaluating key threats is an aspect in which audit should have considerable expertise. It is therefore well placed to review and comment on this phase of the project.

Audit will be looking to ensure that the full and likely range of risks has been considered as well as thought having been given to the more unlikely risks that could eventuate. These latter risks might be those predicted or predicated on risks that might happen if things progress beyond their normal pattern. For example, winds or tides could be higher or demand could drop drastically for the organization's key product or service.

Once the risks have been established and documented they need to be applied to the various business objectives and their components. It is essential that the same risks are applied to all sectors and that no 'allowances' are made. For example, if a power outage is assumed, it must apply equally to all functions in that location and any others that are directly connected to it.

It is also true to say that for every threat there is an opportunity. In undertaking the risk assessment it may be that the project team uncovers some positive results once they factor in the risks. These would need to be fed back into the business in case there are opportunities or directions that could be exploited to the benefit of the organization.

Consider the major newspaper publishing organization that has decided that rather than have business continuity arrangements for its printing works it will rely only on its insurance. This way, if there is an incident, it will not have invested in rebuilding its old systems but will be able to review the situation at that time and then, if appropriate, acquire new state-of-the-art facilities.

The type of positive results that might occur include:

* providing continuity management, continuity support or consultancy to others as a result of going through this process;
* having recognized significant weaknesses in a system, the organization has dealt with issues immediately and thus reduced the further likelihood of that system failing;
* recognizing that there will be supply problems (e.g. in electricity) might offer the organization an opportunity to develop products using alternative technologies;
* changing supply lines might reduce risk of disruption and provide a cost saving;
* bringing services in-house (or outsourcing them) to change the organization's risk profile;
* raising the awareness of risks might create a better culture in the workplace and provide for safer and better controlled business operations.

Analysing risk is looked at in Appendix 2. There is also a matrix indicating how risk could be categorized. This helps to establish an understanding of the different levels of risk that could eventuate and how some are more acceptable than others. Taking that premise one stage further it also enables organizations to determine what could be classed as 'catastrophic' risk – the level where the effect of the risk identified eventuating is greater than the organization could carry.

The length of time that a reduced activity level would be sustainable needs to be arrived at through calculation and not guesswork. In particular the project team may need to consider, with the business activity owners, any events that could have a bearing on how quickly the business needs to be recovered at certain times of the year. This might avoid the organization needing to develop impact assessments and recovery plans for (say) a summer activity where a business failure happened at the end of the season.

Some ideas for an audit scope to review this aspect include:

- determining the adequacy of the risk analysis undertaken;
- evaluating insurance arrangements.

Interdependencies

When identifying and assessing the likely impacts to its business and services the organization must be aware that the impact may not be just on the business and its services, but perhaps on its staff, customers, suppliers and the public. The impact, however, may be two-way in that while problems with the organization could disrupt others, problems with others could disrupt the organization.

This necessitates the project team taking a wide view of the risks identified and applying this to the components of the supply chain, staff and end customers, as well as others who may be involved, or linked, even by accident.

This situation arises where, for example, an organization has had to evacuate its premises but still needs to be in a convenient location for its staff, customers and suppliers to access it. Regrouping the organization to a remote location outside its normal trading area is not going to be a realistic option.

Where the organization has a sole distributor, supplier or provider of its business services there is clearly a risk if that distributor should be forced to suspend trading. The organization may then feel the need to change its contract or take other steps to enable it to mitigate such an exposure.

A related aspect is where any problems with an outsourced service or function might not necessarily show up in the organization straightaway, but could have an eventual knock-on effect. This may be a service disruption, but it might also be the result of an outsourcer running down a contract that has been terminated. In this situation it is possible that the outsourcer may not consider it worth providing the best possible service during the run-down period. The organization clearly needs to manage this aspect closely as it is its reputation that is on the line.

Audit view

Although the project team will identify most of these issues from a straightforward review of business functions and extrapolation of the likely risks, there is still a need to ensure that all the organization's contracts are checked. This is to ensure that none of these dependencies has been overlooked and that the organization is not at risk from some other company's failings.

Audit needs to challenge the assumptions and extrapolations made in this regard to ensure that they have been pragmatic and taken a realistic view.

Performance evaluation and monitoring

Throughout all these processes there is the overriding need to document findings and actions, including why specific options were selected. Where decisions have been taken to exclude factors, these should also be recorded.

All of this documentation needs to be retained as part of the project team's records and to be safeguarded as necessary given that much of it will be highly sensitive.

The processes of recording and storing this information need to recognize that this material will be consulted and updated in the future as systems, needs and risks change. The project team must therefore use clear and unambiguous language along with a minimal level of jargon to enable others to understand their work.

It may be that updates to the documentation continue to be the responsibility of any team that follows the project team but equally this role may fall to individual managers. Either way, the information must be easily retrievable by those with appropriate need and authority.

Audit view

These background papers are often an essential part of an audit review as they show the thinking behind the project. This is vital to a full understanding of the project and is the only way to obtain this knowledge where an audit takes place after the event when memories are hazy or the key players may have moved on.

Finding and retrieving the documentation some time after the project has been concluded may well be tricky especially if the information is not indexed that well or has been archived to some remote location, perhaps making managers reluctant to retrieve it. Audit therefore has another responsibility as part of any review and that is to ensure usability of the documentation by others.

5

Developing the business continuity strategy

Setting the scene

Working with a policy and within a predefined framework, the organization has now garnered enough information to be aware of its assets and the risks that face them. This chapter looks at setting the strategy on how, what and when to recover business functions in the event of an incident.

References

ISO/IEC 22301, clauses 8.3.1, 8.3.2, 8.3.3.

PDCA model

This chapter forms part of the Do (implement and operate) phase of the business continuity life cycle.

Implement and operate the business continuity policy, controls, processes and procedures.

Introduction

The business continuity strategies should be flexible enough to cater for a wide variety of incidents, from complete destructive loss of the organization's business premises, through temporary loss of access – either to premises or to vital facilities – to loss of key members of staff or suppliers. The primary objective is to create a set of documented procedures to facilitate the recovery of the business or business units within predetermined time frames so that the organization's critical functions can be maintained. The strategy development therefore involves understanding the available alternatives (including insurance and mitigation as recovery strategies), their advantages and disadvantages, and all costs that may be relevant.

While individual business units may have a view of their particular recovery and resource requirements, it is not uncommon to find that the sum of all the parts may be greater than the existing whole. Accordingly, a diplomatic tactic of discussing the issues and perhaps downsizing requirements to match available resources may be called for. In such circumstances, it is vital to develop consensus among business units. This will be made easier if there is a universal and clear understanding of the objectives of the business continuity process.

Alternatively, there are occasions when the resources will legitimately be larger for a given recovery than for normal business activity. This will be in situations where the organization needs to work extra hard to retain customers or to work quickly to restore trading. Possible areas in which this could occur include call centres that need additional staff to reassure customers, and trading environments where all staff are focused on customers and cash flow with back-office services taking second place. In these situations, it is likely that the additional resources will show up as temporary measures or perhaps as staff transferred in from other areas.

The project team should be aware of the length of time that business functions can be out of action before it is no longer practical or possible to recover them. This time is known as the maximum tolerable period of disruption, and should be established for each activity through the work conducted during the business impact analysis.

The period of time from when the incident starts to the latest time that the business function can be recovered is the recovery time objective. This will be shorter than the maximum tolerable period of disruption, otherwise recovery will be continuing after the business activity has ceased to be able to operate. With the recovery time objective established, it should then be possible to work back to determine what resources are required to achieve the recovery in that timescale. The faster the recovery then generally the more costly it will be.

When a viable strategy has been developed, the project manager should discuss and agree the proposed strategy with the business heads and project sponsor or sponsors. This avoids surprises, awkward situations and issues further down the line, perhaps in the midst of a real recovery.

Audit view

Internal audit needs to be aware of the continuity strategies as it is itself a function within the organization that may need recovery, and also to review the decisions taken and challenge where any assumptions look unrealistic or inappropriate.

The primary purpose of the audit review is to ensure that the business continuity strategy is intending to recover the organization in a realistic and useful way. The whole organization cannot be resurrected on the day after the incident; it needs to be recovered gradually and with due regard to what needs to be done and in what order.

In this context, the priority of each of the business tasks and their dependencies need to drive the sequence in which the business units are recovered. The number of staff and the jobs that need to be carried out will determine the way the recovery staff numbers start and grow over time. Finally the external dependencies will need to be slotted in to ensure that facilities, supplies, support and all the other aspects of an operating business are in the right place at the right time ready to support the appropriate number of staff.

Many managers will have a view as to how important they, and their business function, are to the organization's objectives, but only top management can decide on the recovery priorities and where (or if) any of those priorities should be revised to achieve some other outcome. Top management will be advised in this by the project team and the signed-off recovery time objective and maximum tolerable period of disruption forecasts for each activity.

Audit will need to review the confidence that can be had in the maximum tolerable period of disruption estimates, as these will have a significant bearing on the recovery time forecasts. If the maximum tolerable period of disruption estimates are best guesses and not based on justifiable facts, then some allowance will need to be made for this to ensure that the recovery time is achieved with time to spare.

Internal audit will also need to vet the documented recovery strategy and assumptions closely to ensure that the organization is being recovered in the way and in the timescale that is necessary for it to continue in business bearing mind there may be regulatory or sectoral issues that could also affect this.

Internal audit also needs to be aware of the situations where more resources are required for recovery than are needed in the ongoing operation. Because, in most cases, the peak needs will be handled by temporary staff and transferees from other locations, it should be relatively straightforward to determine where the need for extra staff is legitimate. Managers may otherwise be tempted to inflate their own staff and resource needs, expecting these figures to be cut back by management in any case.

A useful audit scope for reviewing the development of business continuity strategies is to assess the adequacy and effectiveness of selected strategies in the business continuity policy in the light of the results of the completed business impact analysis process.

Specialist areas

It is so easy to overlook many of the basic requirements in a recovery. The range of permutations may be wide depending upon the nature of the organization.

The following are the basic components that most organizations will need to assess:

- people – staff and others;
- finance;
- buildings and premises;
- telephone and telecommunication systems;
- computers, printers and networks;
- information and data;
- heat, light and power;
- stationery and other disposable stocks;
- goods or services inbound for processing;
- goods or services outbound after processing.

Most organizations will have a combination of these functions, although not all will necessarily be in one location or even operated directly by that organization.

One aspect that relatively few organizations will have are laboratories and in particular those involved in any form of testing dangerous or sensitive materials or animals.

Laboratories in general may require specialist recovery plans because of the additional risks of the chemicals and materials used, as well as potential contamination or loss of the experiments and research in progress. Scientists also rely heavily on their laboratory records to support their results so although much of this will now be computerized there is additional pressure here on assessing the needs of any paper records.

Laboratories involved in animal testing already have significant issues with security and control of animals. They also present more of a target for deliberate action against them than do ordinary laboratories. In the event of an incident, the fact that animal testing takes place there may become common knowledge and could provoke hostile action ultimately leading to the collapse of the organization.

Audit view

Internal audit needs to be acutely aware of any aspects of the organization that make it different from the mainstream and therefore will require some specialist form of recovery expertise or approach to ensure that the plans prepared are robust and that recovery, using those plans, will be effective. It may be difficult, but audit does need to be prepared to challenge the project team at the highest level if they feel that the recovery plans or proposals for any part of the organization fall short of the ideal.

People

The purpose of the exercise is to capture staff numbers in each function and understand what the key roles are. This will enable the project team to propose realistic recovery options with appropriate numbers of staff and the resources that they need to perform their tasks.

Not all staff may be needed in a recovery situation and a pragmatic view is needed with regard to the space, cost and ease of bringing in sufficient staff to maintain the business rather than bringing in all staff just in case.

Consider the international trading floor of a major bank. It has 300 traders but there is only provision for 10 in its immediate recovery location. That is the number it feels is necessary to keep the business going. The remaining traders will be disbursed to offices around the world and will therefore be coming on-stream as the recovery is progressing.

Staff attending in the aftermath of an incident are also going to need facilities like toilets, water, electricity and other services. These requirements can only be properly gauged and sized when the total staff numbers are known.

Staff not brought in immediately as part of the recovery process still need to be involved and kept informed. Gradual take-up of staff may be planned as the organization recovers, but staff need to know this. They need to be kept updated or they may become disillusioned and decide that there will no longer be a job for them to go back to and so seek another one. If this happens it potentially creates a shortage of skilled staff during the later recovery phases.

To help with recovering critical job functions in the aftermath of an incident it may be useful to ensure that at least two staff can perform each critical task, as it cannot be assumed that the incident will happen to a convenient timetable or need. A critical job holder may well be on holiday, off sick or even incapacitated during the incident. Consideration therefore needs to be given to how such a situation will be handled.

One of the risks that needs to be faced is the complete loss of personnel in a business function or the loss of a number of key staff who are travelling together. These risks need to be considered and, if they will realistically affect the organization and its business objectives, mitigating factors or recovery arrangements need to be developed.

Where organizations have remote workers or more mobile staff who do not need access to the main locations very often, their activities need to be coordinated under the plan to ensure that they are not committing the organization to tasks or activities that it cannot fulfil in the aftermath of an incident.

Audit view

The nature of an incident is such that staff, and others involved with the organization, will hear about the incident in different ways. The most likely ways are:

- by official information cascade as staff are alerted through the recovery programme;
- by being on site at the time;
- by arriving on site afterwards;
- by news bulletin or newspaper;
- by word of mouth.

The rise of social media will also play an important part in this, as information is circulated much more quickly than before. With the advent of web-based newspapers, blogs and social media sites, not only is the news available quicker but it will be accompanied by comments and opinion from ordinary people and not from those in the media who are likely to seek to confirm the story before publication. Pictures, especially from mobile cameras, will also be more freely circulated and posted to sites where they can be seen by thousands.

The documented plan needs to recognize these avenues and provide appropriate strategies to deal with those affected. This may include a staff contact point or a feed into the organization's media handling process to issue reassuring and instructional messages to staff and others. Internal audit needs to ensure that this is the case.

A useful side review that may be conducted by the project team or internal audit is to audit the skills that existing staff have but do not use in their normal jobs. This may enable certain staff to be given other tasks during the recovery that fill important or strategic gaps and may reduce any dependency on staff training or using temporary or co-opted workers. The type of skills that may be in demand could include:

- first-aid training;
- prior experience in functions or skills that can be used elsewhere in the organization;
- leadership or management skills, especially within business recovery;
- training or media skills that may be useful to help or inform others;
- salvage and recovery operations.

Where the incident happens during working hours staff need to be given the freedom and facilities to contact their family to reassure them that they are unharmed or unaffected. Where this is not the case the organization has the responsibility to contact relatives to notify them of what has happened. Audit therefore needs to be sure that up-to-date contact lists for staff's relatives are also available as part of the recovery documentation.

There may also be the need for audit to ensure that training and awareness is in place to provide guidance to staff and to offer counselling and support to staff and others who may be traumatized or otherwise affected as a result of the incident. This may generate a separate audit review of the human resources function to determine the level of support available.

Where the incident happens away from the organization but to some of its key players, and that affects the business operation, there may still be a need for counselling and support but perhaps on a more localized scale. Audit needs to ensure that the organization recognizes any obligations that it may have in this event.

Another aspect for audit to consider is whether any of the arrangements put in place to enable staff to perform basic tasks during the recovery phase will compromise the security of the organization either at that time or later. This may happen if staff are given access to confidential or sensitive data without the normal access controls, staff are co-opted to perform tasks outside their normal job functions or temporary workers are drafted in to take some of the load.

Table 10 highlights a selection of the issues that need to be covered at this stage.

Table 10 Personnel recovery issues

Issue	Yes	No	Don't know
Does the business function have a plan for keeping essential employees at work and for the orderly departure of non-essential employees?			
Do key staff understand their role in helping the business function and the organization get back on its feet?			
Does the organization have sufficient food and other necessary provisions to sustain essential employees who must stay at, or return to, work after an incident to get computer and other vital systems operating?			
Is there a plan for the orderly return of various employee groups?			
Do employees have proper identification that will give them access to office locations?			
Has the organization planned a debriefing procedure and professional guidance for distressed employees?			
Have people been designated to report injuries, deaths, damage and needed resources to the appropriate authorities, including the emergency services and employees' families?			

Issue	Yes	No	Don't know
Do staff know how to escalate an incident?			
Do staff know how to react to an incident?			
Do staff know where to get advice, information and/or guidance in an incident?			
Do staff know who is in charge at the time of an incident?			
Have any staff been given specific roles in the event of an incident?			
Are all staff trained in evacuation?			
Are there arrangements to cover staff with critical and unique skills?			

Finance

As a result of the incident, an organization may need to purchase additional materials or obtain services to support or enable the recovery. There may be contracts in place for some of these aspects and arrangements for invoicing but other items will require immediate purchase and expenditure.

Whatever the situation is, the organization has an obligation to maintain good financial controls through an incident. This may include:

- availability of funds for emergency purchases required for response and recovery;
- recording of expenses during an incident.

The incident team will need to be authorized to deal with these matters. This may be through the use of special credit cards or a credit line set up for continuity purposes, using normal company credit cards (where held) or perhaps even through the team's own resources. There ideally should also be some type of cash float for smaller, more immediate purposes.

It is also necessary that the incident team log these costs and retain receipts or other proof of expenditure for later. To facilitate this, there ought to be some appropriate stationery included in the recovery documentation.

Audit view

Although this aspect of strategy may seem pedantic, it is included to ease the burden of the recovery team and to reduce the risks of problems with the tax and other authorities after the incident.

The incident team will be under enough stress without having to worry whether they can afford a hot drink for the recovery team or a taxi fare home for an anxious employee. It is therefore worth considering these kinds of expenditure plus any other likely items before the event.

Audit needs to be aware that, while it needs to ensure that the audit trails and paperwork are in place, it nevertheless needs to recognize that certain actions that might be outside the norm are going to be undertaken during an incident. While it should be on the lookout for inappropriate actions or even fraud, it should also be looking first for any explanations that seem reasonable before determining further actions.

Premises

For the majority of major incidents the building or location that houses the organization, or part of it, is going to be affected. The situation, however, may be that the building is unsafe for some reason or that access to it is prevented by some other factor.

The plan and strategy need to reflect this and the eventuality that any backup records or documentation held in that location are not going to be accessible. This is why the project team has to devise an approach where the plans are available elsewhere, as discussed earlier.

Where premises are unavailable there needs to be a clear plan to ensure that relevant staff, records and processing requirements are relocated. The organization may therefore choose to:

- relocate to its other offices or buildings, where possible;
- borrow, under a contract negotiated in advance, another location;
- use a fully or partially functional, dedicated backup location.

Essentially these three options represent different levels of preparedness and cost. They will also reflect the type of organization involved, as only larger ones are likely to have multiple properties or pockets deep enough to support a dedicated backup location. The different types of dedicated recovery sites are discussed in Chapter 6.

Smaller organizations are likely to rely on reciprocal arrangements with others or with simply keeping backup copies of critical data at another location to ensure that they can at least recover part, if not all, of their business. Alternatively, they may opt for having their key staff working from home and communicating electronically or by telephone. This way, the business will continue operating, albeit on a smaller scale.

Home, remote and mobile workers will not be as greatly affected by loss of any office premises but nevertheless their needs have to be taken into consideration. This may require a greater emphasis on a technological solution than might otherwise be required early in a recovery plan.

The recovery time objective will have an impact upon all decisions about premises and their usage. Although there are many permutations of solution, the following examples illustrate the points.

- Where the recovery time objective is long, say several months, then there may be no need to take any action but to simply await the end of the interruption and any remedial action required at that site.
- Where the recovery time objective is medium term, say two months or less, there should be time to relocate staff and resources and to recover the operation. This may require displacement of staff or lower priority activities at the new location.
- Where the recovery time objective is very short, say less than a day, there may be insufficient time to move staff and other facilities but simply time enough to transfer the functions required to other locations – assuming the capacity is there. This could be where home working comes to the fore.

Costs will also be a determinant in choices made.

A potential matrix to determine relocation options against the identified recovery time period could be developed using the example in Table 11. This will need to reflect available premises, equipment and other recovery needs at those locations.

Table 11 Summary of relocation strategies against recovery time

	In-house solutions that can be invoked to provide recovery	Recovery solutions that have been contracted out	Shortfalls and how they will be dealt with
Estimated recovery period – Immediate			
Estimated recovery period – Hours			
Estimated recovery period – Days			
Estimated recovery period – Weeks			
Estimated recovery period – Months			

Audit view

Internal audit needs to challenge the assumptions in the plan very carefully. In particular it needs to look at the logistics of the move, the likelihood of events happening and the availability of staff, knowledge and records to make the transfer to another location something that will keep the business running.

At one time it was considered appropriate for buildings on one site to be used as a backup for each other, providing they were a reasonable distance apart. It is unlikely now that many organizations would feel that such a short distance would be reasonable. Emergency services tend to cordon off areas within a square kilometre after explosions and other significant incidents. Indeed, multinational organizations are used to thinking in terms of off-country backup and recovery relationships rather than just off site.

The approach adopted by some financial organizations, and one that provides a useful rule of thumb, is that the recovery site should be at least 10 kilometres away but still easily accessible for staff, customers and suppliers (as appropriate) as these may be fundamental to keeping the business going.

Depending on the recovery location the organization may need to provide some form of staff transport to alleviate parking or other travel problems and ensure that staff can reach the site. If this is the case then this needs to be factored into the plan and any contracts or other agreements to guarantee the service should be put in place.

In the event of a loss of the building or access to it there may be the need for the organization to outsource some of its operations. Again this should be recognized in the plan and formalized with contracts or other agreements.

One of the main aspects for audit to review is whether the organization has sole occupancy of any remote recovery locations. If this is not the case then the plan needs to be reviewed in the light of:

- whether the other player(s) are in the same location as the organization and therefore potentially susceptible to the same incident;
- whether there are any plans in place at the recovery site to segregate the two (or more) organizations both in terms of recovery space, support services and security;
- what the priority is if all organizations contracted to use the site wish to do so at the same time.

Clearly there is scope for problems with this arrangement and audit must ensure that the organization is not put at risk through any compromises on its recovery location. Audit should also ensure that, if the organization has separate recovery plans, each plan is not expecting to use the same recovery location at the same time.

If the organization is using a known recovery location then audit should inspect the building, its location and services. This is to ensure that it is not vulnerable to the same sort of problems or some others that are equally likely to occur.

Consider the financial organization who allocated space in one of its buildings for a treasury recovery site. The space was fully equipped and ready to take all the dealers and allow them to carry on working. The problem, highlighted by an audit, was that the recovery site was on the ground floor of a building on the flood plain outside the Thames Barrier. It could therefore have been flooded in the event the barrier was raised to protect London.

In some cases the plans will have to call for forward planning and expenditure on backup and recovery locations that can take the load – or at least some of it – in the event of an incident. Clearly this is very much in the nature of an insurance against which the organization will hope never to claim. Consequently, the facilities provided for recovery are likely to be such that they neither are a drain on the organization nor are able to wholly duplicate the primary location they are acting as a recovery site for.

Financial services is one of the sectors where expenditure on 'hot' recovery sites is often justified. A hot recovery site is one where everything is ready for immediate use (see Chapter 6). The reason for this is that the amount of money traded in a few minutes could well exceed the cost of establishing and maintaining a recovery site. Based on such a calculation the decision is clear cut.

It may not be such an easy calculation for other organizations and sectors where set-up and running costs are not so easily and quickly recovered. Many organizations will turn to outsourcers to provide these facilities as this approach tends to defray the costs across the customer base of the outsourcer.

Technology

Managing the technology side of any recovery can be very difficult due to the diversity of systems and especially their interconnectivity.

Consider the hospital that did not realize that many of its operating room systems were indirectly connected to the internet. As they did not appreciate this risk they did not take steps to mitigate it by installing firewalls and other controls. They were therefore shocked when several operating rooms had to be shut down because of a computer virus.

Increasingly organizations are relying on third-party suppliers and trading partners to supply data or programs or to undertake some degree of information processing. In some cases entire organizations are founded on the electronic services or links provided by others. In these cases the risks may come from outside or inside the organization, but if they lead to supply or service disruption they will need a coherent recovery plan. This is far more difficult to document and implement, as there may be many recovery permutations.

Consider the organization that had established two separate power supplies to its headquarters. It was therefore very surprised to have a total power outage. Investigations showed that a worker drilling the road some way away had broken through the cables a metre or so after the two separate power supplies had come together in one conduit.

A similar problem arises with dark sites where the lack of any IT resource means that the recovery team are trying to understand the reasons for a problem and trying to effect a recovery, all from some considerable distance away. The problems of company X mentioned in Chapter 1 illustrate some of the simpler issues that can occur.

The geographical spread of the IT function can cause additional problems but can also potentially increase the resilience of the whole system. Distributed processing, where the key processing activities occur in different locations, can help to provide stability for organizations that need such an approach. Electronic vaulting, where backup copies of the data are stored in remote off-site locations, and real-time backups across networks, can help restore systems that are subject to a local failure.

The complete loss of a data centre could be catastrophic for an organization if all its backups and fallback options exist in or around that building. This is one of the potential problems for small organizations, as they will probably only have one site for all business activities.

The loss of electronic mail and telecommunications systems can have a significant impact upon remote and out-of-office workers, as well as clients and trading partners.

Key machines and systems may need to be given particular protection, both physical and logical, in order to ensure that they are not tampered with and do not suffer outages caused by unexpected events, such as power cuts, computer viruses, disgruntled staff and other issues.

Consider the organization that made several key staff redundant. The staff did not have their ID badges and building access revoked at the time of the redundancy announcement. They entered the headquarters building after hours and destroyed a key server involved in processing crucial data for the project they were working on. Because this was a unique machine a new one had to be ordered, delaying the project by over a month.

The lead time in getting a replacement in the above example shows why it is necessary to plan ahead in ensuring that all essential equipment is available when needed. It is also worth appreciating that equipment suppliers regularly update and change the hardware and the software they offer as part of their sales and marketing approaches. Similarly, suppliers and the markets might move away from a previously favoured product to something new. These aspects might have particular consequences for an organization needing to recover data to a new system that is no longer compatible with the software or data traditionally used in the organization.

Some organizations do not feel the need to regularly move old data to new machines and software, as this can be a long and time-consuming process. It can also be costly and a waste of time and resources if the data is merely to be stored again and not used. Instead they retain at least one example of all the old hardware and software so that the data can be recovered in future if it is needed. If this situation is found in the organization then the recovery plan may need to reflect it depending on how valuable the old data is and whether it is likely to be required in the recovery phase.

Audit view

Internal audit must ensure that the IT function has provided the project team with an up-to-date list of all the connections that the organization has to third party and other bodies. Assumptions have to be made that every one of these systems poses a risk to the organization that needs to be managed. During recovery some of these systems may need to be reduced in capability, not recovered at all or used in very controlled circumstances in order to prevent them causing further potential problems.

Totally in-house systems must also be identified to ensure that they are not accidentally connected to an externally facing system during the recovery phase, as they may lack the protection to deal with the risks external connectivity poses.

Software audits, which were discussed in Chapter 4, contribute to the understanding of whether users within the organization not only utilize the same software but also the same version. Restricting the options of software used and the version simplifies support and transfer of information around the organization. Corruption of data when moved between systems and other media can also be a significant problem.

Although the main thrust of the audit will be to review the work of the project team there are also potentially other areas that need to be considered. This will include new and ongoing projects and initiatives that may affect the future smooth running of the organization and its business operations.

Consider the case of the financial organization that outsourced development of a major customer-facing system. The outsourcers included some trial software rather than the full copy that should have been used in the pilot roll-out to six locations. Shortly after this, the trial software timed out and the software stopped functioning. This happened at 11.00 a.m. on a Saturday on the day that annual interest was added to most of the accounts – the busiest day of the year.

Overall therefore, internal audit has a lot of areas that it needs to consider when assessing technological recovery. It cannot afford to be led by the project team or the IT function but needs to reassure itself that the solutions proposed are reasonable, viable and appropriate. In some circumstances, and depending on the technical knowledge within the audit team, this may warrant audit involving external advisers to validate the findings and approaches adopted.

Any additional technological needs arising out of the provision of one or more continuity plans should be consolidated as far as possible to ensure that commonality of equipment is obtained, where appropriate, and that costs are reduced through volume purchase.

Information

Information is the lifeblood of any organization and as such all information assets should be safeguarded. While equipment, premises and even to some extent people can be replaced without greatly impacting the organization, the loss of its data can be crippling. It is therefore necessary to take strong precautions to ensure that as a result of an incident:

- data existing within the organization is given a very high degree of protection, recovery ability and security;
- data recovered after an incident is treated in the same way even though there will be considerable pressure to treat it with less security given the difficult circumstances and the inevitable shortcuts that are being taken during that time.

In general terms security is perceived as providing protection for something. However, in order to understand its ramifications and implications it is useful to break it down into its three key components:

Confidentiality

Providing protection from unauthorized access or disclosure.

Integrity

Ensuring that systems and information are complete and free from unauthorized change or modification.

Availability

Ensuring that information, services and resources are available when and where required.

It is normal to consider all three elements applying to every piece of information held and to every transaction undertaken.

An aspect that has received an increasing amount of attention in the past few years is privacy and especially personal privacy. Systems and processes designed to achieve this place considerable emphasis on the importance of confidentiality in protecting personal information. It is, however, not the only aspect. The integrity of the data has to be maintained to ensure that the data shown is correct, while the availability covers the delivery of the data to the right person at the right time. Clearly, out-of-date, amended information sent to the wrong person is a problem no matter how well protected the source information was.

Most organizations will have a baseline level of security that applies to all resources. It is the degrees of security implemented beyond this that could be regarded as discretionary based on the sensitivity and value of the data and information that is being protected. During business recovery it is important not to breach these baseline and discretionary security levels as this could put the recovery, and the organization, at risk.

Some of the information that may need to be accessed during a recovery may require special equipment. The plan needs to reflect this and ensure that such equipment is available and working at the recovery location.

Where information is stored in remote locations but is available electronically, perhaps through a provision for electronic vaulting or from a dark site unaffected by the incident, then the data can be accessed through a network set up in the recovery location. If this is the case it needs to be ensured that the recovery network does not expose the organization to any new or greater risks than were the case at the original location.

Because of the lack of certainty of having networks and electronic systems up and running at the time of an incident, it is necessary to have the continuity plans available in hard copy. Other key recovery documents may also be held in hard copy along with information that staff have in their possession or can be recovered from the original location. Such information is valuable and needs to be safeguarded. Provision may therefore need to be made in the recovery plan to secure sensitive documents.

Audit view

In framing its views on this aspect of the continuity plan, audit should have regard for ISO/IEC 27001 and 27002, which deal with information security. These standards provide useful information on how security systems can be developed and managed.

There may, however, be a need to provide other safeguards, such as ensuring that information printed out is only available to those that need to know. It should also be ensured that there are facilities at the recovery location to shred sensitive and other material that the organization may not want broadcast widely.

There is also no harm in considering the issues of information protection in a much wider context. Most organizations have a clear desk policy. The idea is to ensure that all information is kept out of sight except when in use. Overnight, there should not be any data left out. Clearly, this protects information from prying eyes and visitors but also, in the event of an explosion or where a building has to be evacuated, it limits the information that will be blown off desks, out of the windows or that will become available to any unauthorized person who enters the building.

As part of its annual reassurance programme, internal audit may have carried out an audit on information assets. This will have yielded details of the nature of data flows as well as where key information is held and stored. It will also show the backup plans and off-site storage arrangements. All of this information should be reflected in the recovery plan, as it establishes the way the organization is being run and where data and information are available.

Recovering data and information from a storage location is always considerably easier and poses fewer risks than information that has to be rebuilt from odd records and notes made by staff and users.

If the incident is computer-related, such as a computer virus, many of the larger databases that organizations use to hold significant data can be rolled back to a point before the incident and thus enable recovery from clean data. Clearly this would require information added after the incident to be rebuilt but at least it will only represent a relatively small amount of work and therefore a lower risk than having to rebuild all the data. Use of backup media would achieve a similar result for other IT systems.

Audit should also be ensuring that the recovery plan reflects the priorities of the organization when it looks at data recovery. There is no value in spending time and effort recovering data that will not be required in the recovery schedule for some time while leaving urgently needed information unrecovered or out of date. This is especially true when the organization's first priority is to make use of that data, such as invoicing customers in order to keep the cash flow going.

Internal audit should also have a view on how the recovery information is made available. Traditional 'battle boxes' are available in some organizations, containing the key recovery documents in paper format, whereas others have set up web locations where this data is held. Each of these options, plus most of the variations in between, have pros and cons and audit needs to take a serious look at the issues involved for its own organization. This is discussed further in Chapter 7.

Supplies

Rather like information, supplies need to be of the correct type and in the right place to have any value. The plan therefore needs to reflect this and to highlight any particular, or peculiar, supply needs or supply arrangements.

One of the most critical might perhaps be the 'just-in-time' arrangements that manufacturers often employ. This means that suppliers are obliged to deliver precise quantities to an agreed schedule, which means the manufacturing organization does not need to maintain much, if any, spare stock. Clearly, if the incident affects the manufacturing facility and the work has to be transferred elsewhere, this will disrupt the just-in-time arrangements and may require the organization to hold more interim stock – if that is possible. Similarly, the supplier will need to know the effect on that business as it too may have just-in-time or other less-flexible arrangements. Once recovery is underway then the just-in-time arrangements can be reintroduced at the new site if appropriate.

On the same lines, if the incident is at the supplier and the organization ceases to receive the goods and supplies it expects then this could create a knock-on incident. Where this is a risk the recovery plan needs to recognize it and put in place options, such as other suppliers who can source at short notice, holding a reserve stock as a disaster recovery option, or perhaps slowing down production to cope with available stocks. Stopping or slowing the production process is not a good outcome but may be the expedient option.

For warehouse and other large storage operations the problems raised are not so different depending on the incident. Where the warehouse receives goods and this supply is disrupted then there will be a knock-on effect upon the warehouse distribution arrangements. The same will apply, at least in the short term, when it is the warehouse that is affected.

Recovering a warehouse, like a factory, is a large undertaking and requires detailed forward planning. Organizations may therefore choose to outsource some, or all, of their production, storage or distribution services in the immediate aftermath of an incident. This will provide time while the new facilities are brought on-stream. Alternatively, the organization may make arrangements with its key customers that while there will be disruption in supply after an incident, providing it is contained to a limited period while the recovery facilities get up and running, it may be acceptable and not lead to loss of contracts.

Where the supplies are not particularly visible, such as telecommunications and power, the business recovery project team might recommend the use of two suppliers for each to spread the risk.

Telecommunications and power will also be required at any recovery location. The project team should arrange these in advance but there may need to be some form of switchover to these backup services in the event of the plan being invoked. The arrangements for this would need to be detailed in the plan.

The recovery site will also require more basic supplies, such as stationery. The team should identify the minimum needs for this and when they will be required during the recovery phases. Any specialized forms or documents would need to be specified and ordered in advance because of the lead time involved. It may be that for a short period the organization uses easily available stationery rather than anything special in order to simplify and speed the recovery.

Audit view

Internal audit will be concerned that the organization's recovery plans extend to safeguarding the supplies that are necessary to get an operation going and keep it supplied. The services can be anything from telecommunications through stationery to perishable goods or metalworking tools. The issues, however, remain the same: the organization needs these items and will not be able to continue operation without them.

In some cases special arrangements and contracts will need to be issued to provide this material, perhaps in partnership with other contracts to provide other aspects of the recovery. In other cases it may be necessary to order or arrange for additional material over and above the normal requirements to help stock a recovery site.

If the latter is the case, then some thought needs to be given to the storage locations and whether they are suitable for the purpose.

Consider the situation in a government-funded body. To reduce the costs on the public purse a senior employee ordered three years' worth of stationery including envelopes. These were stored on the site in an unused former industrial building – an old railway engine shed. Within a year the envelopes were so damp they had to be thrown away along with lots of the other items.

Storage suitability is not just related to the conditions (temperature, humidity, magnetic fields and so on) but should also take into account the security of the items and the ability to get access to them when required. Extending beyond that it should also be considered whether the storage space involved could be used for a better purpose, including becoming part of a business operation for the organization.

For many of the items required there will be a lead time involved. This also needs to be built into the plan to ensure that items are requested at appropriate times. There may also be delivery restrictions depending on the location and access to the recovery site.

To provide a level of support to IT and other electrical equipment it may be necessary to install or hire a generator. These are often intended for short-term use to fill the need during a power outage and may not always be suitable for long-term use.

Consider the utility that had a backup generator installed. During an IT disaster recovery test the generator was turned on. At the end of the test it was found impossible to stop it. Simply letting it run out of fuel (it had a two-hour tank capacity) was not an option as this could have adversely affected their IT systems. It took four days to design a solution, go through their change control processes, install the fix and organize an orderly switch over to the main supply. During this period, every two hours, someone had to be there to fill the generator's fuel tank.

Another point to consider is the recovery needs, not just for each business function, but across the whole organization. Audit should ensure that as much as possible of the recovery material and resources that are common across the functions should be purchased through one order. This is both to simplify the process and also to enable negotiation of a better price.

Audit should also be looking at other supplier contracts such as those for software. During a recovery, the organization will need to have access to the software it normally uses. The software it did use may well be buried in another building several kilometres away and totally inaccessible. The organization will not, therefore, wish to re-purchase software it already has acquired simply because it cannot get immediate access to it. Having some form of software site licence would usually provide sufficient flexibility to cover this situation but for other software this may not be the case. There is no standard answer, as this aspect is very much in the hands of the publishers. The reason being that the software continues to belong to the publishers, organizations and users merely purchase a licence to use it. Having the results of a valid and recent software audit to show actual holdings may also be beneficial.

Stakeholders

The various different stakeholders will all be involved to a different degree in the recovery of the organization. Many will be arm's length and require only notification of the incident and perhaps some details of what is happening. Some will require being actively involved.

The primary stakeholders with a direct interest will probably be those involved in supplying the organization, trading with it, looking after its staff members and regulating it. Others, such as shareholders, will be looking at their investment more in terms of profit and loss than in the detailed recovery aspects.

Suppliers have to some extent been considered in the previous section, as they are involved with providing the raw materials that the business needs to operate. Nevertheless they will need to be involved in discussions with the organization both in relation to how they will react to an incident affecting the organization, and also in how any incident affecting them will in turn affect the organization. It may be that all parties work together to develop a common understanding and ensure that there is consistency and mutual support in the continuity plans they develop.

In practice the larger the organization the more likely it is that it can pressurize its suppliers into developing continuity plans as a price of staying a supplier.

Customers are potentially more fickle as they probably have less to gain by committing to stay with an organization that has had to invoke its recovery plan. The organization is therefore more likely to seek to cover this point in its contracts where it can and to try to establish itself as the single source for the buyer's needs. If it can achieve this it will provide some insulation for its position.

Of course where the organization is a supplier it may be that its customer is the one that is forcing the development of a continuity plan as the price of remaining a supplier.

Unions will simply be looking to safeguard their members' interests and welfare and will wish to ensure that the continuity plan reflects this. If it is properly constructed it will do so. Where the continuity plan highlights inappropriate activities or practices that management chooses to change then issues might arise with the union or other members' representatives, but this would be outside the scope of the continuity plan itself.

Local and central government will be concerned to ensure that the incident is managed and contained properly and that invoking the continuity plan does not lead to further problems of breaches of any rules or regulations.

The emergency services will need to be involved to vet any recovery locations for ease of escape and also for recommendations on how such locations can be used safely.

Audit view

Although the project team will identify all these issues it may not be their responsibility to negotiate with the stakeholders to achieve the desired outcomes. There will be a number of people in the organization better placed to perform this delicate task.

In addition, the organization needs to ensure that there are people in place who will take a similar responsibility if an incident occurs that requires the continuity plan to be invoked. At that point the organization will need to gain the trust and support of these stakeholders and to work with them and through them to achieve a satisfactory recovery.

Audit should be aware of these people networks and ensure that those who should be involved are involved. This will be especially relevant if the team developing the business continuity plan is from outside the organization.

Audit scopes to review this aspect include:

- ensuring that appropriate liaison is maintained with external parties;
- ensuring that public and media relations would be effectively addressed during an emergency to minimize adverse publicity and reputation risk.

Outsourcers and their plans

The primary reason for ensuring that outsourcers used by the organization either have their own plans or are linked into the organization's plans is to ensure that the organization's supply of products and services is not disrupted by a failure of a contracted third party.

If the outsourcer is expected to recover their systems outside the organization's continuity plan then the organization needs to be sure that the outsourcer actually has effective and appropriate plans in place.

Audit view

Internal audit should ensure as a matter of priority that the contract between the outsourcer and the organization, or any of its business functions, allows audit to have sufficient access to enable it to undertake reviews and testing across all aspects that impinge upon business continuity and to comment meaningfully on the situation.

Internal audit needs to vet the procedures and processes to ensure that the outsourcer's plans are suitable and meet the business needs. The organization needs to work with the outsourcer to test the plans to make sure that the anticipated meshing of plans or the separate recovery processes will happen as expected.

Audit should be present as an independent observer of these tests and contribute to the feedback on whether and how activities can be improved.

In certain situations, a supplier might have multiple business customers (for example a provider of cloud services) but rather than have audits by each of them it has contracted an independent third party to provide one audit certificate to satisfy them all. Customers are therefore kept at arm's length and are relying on someone else's assurances. Audit should take this issue up with top management if the project team have not already done so, as it could lead to incorrect information or assumptions being made.

Protection and mitigation

In the process of going through these various areas and aspects, the project team should be ever mindful that, rather than simply relying on a recovery of the business, they take active steps to reduce the likelihood of an event happening in the first place. Similarly, wherever possible they should consider if there are any actions that could be taken to reduce the recovery time period and to limit the impacts of disruption.

To help keep the business running smoothly, some of the following aspects may be looked at:

- eliminating single points of failure;
- eliminating bottlenecks in production and supply;
- being aware of the typical mean time before failure (MTBF) figures for any equipment used;
- reviewing comparable organizations and businesses for any potential problem areas or options for improvement;
- undertaking capacity planning to ensure resources match or exceed needs;
- being aware of potential health and safety problem areas;
- monitoring staff and processes to see if there are any obvious weak spots in the way things operate.

Much of this work should be part of the everyday organizational management and there will be people tasked with undertaking these reviews. Nevertheless, the project team will be in a good position to have an overview and therefore perhaps to see connections and ramifications that others may not.

Similarly, the project team might well come across ideas or opportunities that will enable speedier recovery. Perhaps better education of staff, more (or additional) system monitoring or perhaps additional investment in newer equipment that would be more reliable.

Looking at the impacts of any disruption and how these might be reduced is another fruitful area. Again, better education will help but also the organization may decide to invest in backup or spare machinery or equipment. It might be worth cross-training teams so they could support each other if needed. Even increasing the amount of standardization across the organization may bring benefits as equipment, software, staff skills and other things could be used to help another area of the business recovery more quickly.

Audit view

Not only is the project team in a good place to see where some of these matters may be resolved, so too is internal audit. Indeed, to some extent the project team may even be doing audit's work if it can get the organization to improve and streamline its processes.

Figure 5 shows the profile of an incident along with the disruption and recovery phases. Whilst an incident places major stress on the organization, the disruption also causes stress and it is not until the recovery phase that this starts to tail off. A short sharp incident, or one which can be recovered from quickly, obviously produces less stress on the organization and this is the major reason why audit should be supporting any moves there are to reduce impact and recovery times.

Audit does, however, need to be aware that the project team is looking at this from only one perspective – that of easing the recovery burden. Internal audit has a much wider remit and must consider the big picture. To do this, it needs to take account of the impacts of the recommendations and any additional risks that they bring into play. For example, upgrading to newer equipment may give better MTBF figures and faster recoverability but this may be accompanied by more infrastructure spending, an increased training budget and a higher likelihood of staff misusing the asset.

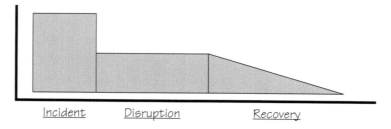

Incident   Disruption   Recovery

Figure 5 Incidence recovery profile

Performance evaluation and monitoring

Management should ensure that they understand and agree with the basis on which the various risks looked at are dealt with. It would be too easy for the risk appetite of the organization to be diverted from its normal range simply because the project team made decisions based on their own assessments rather than those the organization would be comfortable with.

The project team should also be documenting its findings and its thinking in reaching decisions as this may be valuable in the future. This aspect is particularly crucial if the team is one bought in from outside the organization as their ideas and thinking will be lost when they leave.

Audit view

In theory, any person in the organization knowing the risk appetite and having the same facts at their disposal should arrive at the same conclusion. This is the cross-check that internal audit could carry out when vetting decisions made. Unfortunately, there will still have to be a margin for flexibility but, nevertheless, the more information recorded by the project team, the more closely audit will be able to verify and validate their decisions.

One key aspect for internal audit to consider is whether any significant risks have been ignored or overridden by business expediency. For example, other organizations using the same equipment have been experiencing a high rate of failure but this has not, so far, been the case in this organization; so no alternative provisions have been made, enabling the saved budget to be used elsewhere. Whilst this kind of action may, in time, prove to have been a shrewd move, it is also replacing a known risk with an unknown one. In the example above, the known risk is the cost of an alternative whilst the unknown risk is the full impact of any failure, knowing there is no backup option available.

6

Incident recovery

Setting the scene

Knowing its assets and risks and with an agreed strategy in place the organization can now make informed decisions about recovering those assets. It does, however, need to understand what an incident may be like before it can formulate what it may need to deal effectively with one.

References

ISO 22301, clauses: 8.4.1, 8.4.2, 8.4.3.

PDCA model

This chapter forms part of the Check (monitor and review) phase of the business continuity life cycle.

Monitor and review performance against business continuity policy and objectives, report the results to management for review, and determine and authorize actions for remediation and improvement.

Introduction

The first few minutes, hours or days after the incident occurs (depending on its size and severity) can be particularly crucial for any organization.

The incident management team is initially going to be working in a vacuum with relatively little information available and much of that will be confused and garbled. There may be speculation on the incident with hard information just not available.

Clarification may be difficult to obtain, especially if the incident is happening some distance from the incident team or affects the incident team directly.

Consider a major incident, like a bombing, where public services are disrupted and access may be difficult to achieve to assess casualties or damage. Reports will rely on eyewitnesses who are often unreliable – those who see least, often say most.

Consider a localized incident, like a switchboard or computer failure, that prevents the organization from trading and the incident team from receiving any up-to-date information.

With this background of uncertainty the team is still going to have to decide whether to invoke the plan and, if so, which plan (if the organization has more than one) and how much of it to bring into play.

Managing the situation

One model of a command structure for incidents that is used in business continuity recoveries is known as the gold-silver-bronze approach and it is discussed more fully in Appendix 6. In essence, it is a way of defining who has control of the incident and their viewpoint of the incident. Those closest to the incident deal with the tactical issues on the ground, while those furthest away look after the strategic and wider-ranging aspects. This ensures that, as long as there is good communication between those involved, there is a clear definition and responsibility over who is doing what.

While the three levels provide an appropriate model for large and medium-sized organizations with the incident at a single location, a smaller organization or a multiple-site incident may require different approaches. Small organizations may find that one recovery team close to the action is the best approach, while for multiple-site issues perhaps a team at each site operating independently may be more reactive.

For certain incidents, where there is an unknown cause or a serious risk to life, the emergency services will take charge of the incident and the organization's incident team will be relegated to a secondary role.

Audit view

Working out how to deal with an incident in advance is key to a fast and coherent response if an incident does happen. Audit therefore needs to be satisfied that this important aspect has been considered. It should also be clear from audit's review that a variety of risk factors have been used to help determine the different approaches required depending upon the circumstances. For example a fire poses different initial appraisal factors and difficulties compared to a flood or an earthquake. A cordon may be placed round a whole area to seal it in the case of foot and mouth or other communicable diseases. Light and telecommunications may or may not be available. Access may be easy or difficult. There are many unknowns and the initial appraisal approach needs to cope with as many of them as possible.

One approach to capturing data after an incident is summarized by the mnemonic 'SAD CHALETS'. This is shown in Table 12 and may be a useful concept for organizational recovery teams to adopt.

Table 12 Collating information after an incident

Survey	Survey the scene on approach
Assess	Assess the situation on arrival
Disseminate	Disseminate the following information
Casualties	Casualties, approximate numbers of dead, injured and uninjured
Hazards	Hazards present and potential
Access	Best access routes for emergency vehicles
Location	The exact location of the incident
Emergency	Emergency services and other agencies present and required
Type	Type of incident and brief details of number of vehicles, buildings, etc. involved
Safety	All aspects of health and safety and risk assessment must be considered by all staff working at or close to the scene

The response structure must be resilient to as many preconceived problems as possible. This means that audit should test the hypotheses carefully for likely weak spots and information bottlenecks. If the gold-silver-bronze model is being used then audit should ensure that each party knows their responsibilities and their limits. Audit should also ensure that there is appropriate communication backup provided to enable this.

If the incident is large then there will be pressure on fixed and mobile lines as others try to call in or call out. Staff will want to call their relatives and equally relatives will be trying to call in. Emergency services tend to use dedicated frequencies so their communications are less likely to be disrupted, but getting hold of them in the first place may be difficult. If all else fails then members of the recovery team may need to act as runners.

If the incident involves serious damage then there may be no fixed communication lines anyway. There might also be risks arising from the incident that prevent emergency services from reaching the site very quickly, if at all.

A potential alternative is to enlist the help of local amateur radio enthusiasts or their equivalent. The equipment they have may provide an option at locations where communications have been severely disrupted.

It may prove useful to consider the following aspects.

- Provide for communication through channels other than fixed line or mobile phones. Options might include using wireless-based internet-based communications (voice over internet protocol – VOIP), radio sets, couriers or perhaps just resorting to staff or team members carrying messages.
- Ensure that the incident team can be contacted in as many ways as possible and that the emergency services and staff know the contact numbers and contact channels that are appropriate.
- Ensure that the incident team is manned at all times. This means making sure that whatever the time of day or night someone from the incident team can be contacted by the emergency services, staff and others, to receive information about incidents.
  Consider the organization based in a rural location. As they were the largest employer in the area they were automatically notified by the police whenever there were road accidents near their site in case it involved a staff member.
- Ensure that the incident team is actually able to invoke the plan. In many situations the backup site or outsourced supplier will require some form of identification and reference number before they will undertake any work.

By invoking the business continuity plan the organization has declared itself to be having a problem. It is true that the plan should make it a containable problem and one that the organization can recover from. However, suppliers may not take such a view and may be concerned that they will not be paid for any supplies or goods provided. The organization may therefore need to ensure that cash, credit card or bank support, as appropriate, is in place in order to satisfy suppliers and other creditors.

Customers will likewise be concerned about the impact upon them. Where the incident involves people, then there need to be processes available to capture details of who is involved and provide support lines for relatives and friends. Establishing and widely promulgating the number of a dedicated telephone line for concerned relatives and friends to call is one way of achieving this. Information flows will need to be established and ensure that positive messages are given wherever possible. This should also extend to any web or social media presence the organization has.

What to invoke

Determining how much of the plan to invoke is a very subjective issue at the time of the incident. Accurate information will be very hard to come by, while the pressure on the incident team to do something will grow rapidly. Table 13 highlights the relevant types of choices.

Disaster recovery is considered more fully later in this chapter. It is usually a stand-alone process but will also become part of any business continuity programme that is introduced.

In some situations the actions to take will be obvious. If the building is on fire then full evacuation and involvement of the emergency services will be the only choice, but if the incident is less dramatic and perhaps only involves part of the organization then the choices may not be so clear-cut.

Ideally the business continuity plan or the activity response plan will provide some support in this respect, as it might indicate practical issues and possible options. Table 14 portrays a much simplified and theoretical recovery plan index and its links to various processes and documents.

Table 13 Invocation decision matrix

Incident	Incident management plan	Business continuity plan	Activity response plan	Disaster recovery plan
Widespread incident – perhaps a pandemic (No business continuity plan prepared for this eventuality)	Invoked Incident team handle incident			
Major incident – perhaps involving one building and all services in it (Business continuity plan in place for this eventuality)	Invoked ➚	Invoked Business continuity team uses plan to guide recovery		
Major incident – but only one small part of it – perhaps breakdown of air purifiers in a laboratory (Activity response plan in place to guide recovery)	Invoked ➚	Invoked ➚	Invoked Activity response team uses very detailed plans to effect recovery	
Minor incident involving IT systems only (Disaster recovery plan in place)	Invoked ➚	Invoked ➚	&#10132;	Invoked Disaster recovery plan used to guide recovery

NOTE: A disaster recovery plan has been the traditional recovery tool for IT functions for many years. There is, however, no requirement to have this layer of plan title if the organization wishes to standardize on activity response plans as the detailed recovery document.

Table 14 Sample recovery plan action index

Level of incident	Recovery processes
Total loss of building	• Invoke building recovery plan in full
Partial loss of building	• Invoke evacuation processes from building recovery plan – see red pages • Attempt to ascertain cause and any further risks • Contact facilities director to establish recovery steps – contact details in the blue folder • Notify senior executive – contact details in blue folder
Total loss of IT systems	• Invoke IT disaster recovery plan in full • Determine business impact • Invoke business recovery aspects of plan if necessary – see section 6 in green folder
Partial loss of IT systems	• Determine cause and effect • Contact IT director to establish recovery steps – contact details in blue folder • Notify senior executive – contact details in blue folder
Loss of key executive	• Contact most senior available manager and discuss options – contact details in blue folder

Audit view

Audit should be challenging to ensure that the plan can be invoked in stages depending upon the severity and nature of the incident.

To support a staged approach there may need to be an index of actions that the incident team should normally take if given events occur (see Table 14). In addition, the plan could usefully be laid out in sections to facilitate different states of recovery as appropriate to the perceived risks.

It has to be said that if there is an index of actions to be taken by the incident team, then this should be guidance and not prescribed. The reason for this is simply that events won't always follow the laid-down direction and other factors will need to be considered.

Although many plans are designed to facilitate recovery from a major incident, in practice it is often the smaller incidents that create the bigger problems. This is because they are overlooked, or not noticed, and their effects can be cumulative.

Consider the new recruit to a human resources team. When setting up her computer access the IT team had mistakenly given her 'administrator' privileges rather than the very limited access she actually needed. When she accidentally pressed the wrong key combination her computer started to display screens of information that her training had not equipped her to deal with. In an effort to return to something familiar she pressed random keys. This made matters worse. Her actions, however, did succeed in bringing down the entire human resources network as well as other parts of the IT system.

In this context are organizations that allow staff to download unlimited material from the internet. This can cause problems that build up or develop over time:

- users might download inappropriate material, leading the organization to be involved in civil or criminal actions;
- users might download large amounts of data, leading to loss of bandwidth on the network and to faster usage of available storage media;
- users might download illegal or inappropriate software that, when used, causes unexpected results in standard organizational software, brings in viruses and malicious code, opens up the organization to easier penetration by attackers or distributes organizational data outside the organization boundaries.

Some screensaver software is designed to allow remote machines to link together to perform extremely complex tasks. Connecting remote machines in this way is known as grid computing and it is a very powerful tool, but it can mean that machines are communicating through firewalls and other protection devices. If these links are exploited by attackers it renders the organization liable to severe compromise.

Control the incident

Although incidents can be managed they do tend to develop a life of their own and can, if not controlled, lead the incident team in wrong directions. As discussed earlier, the gold-silver-bronze approach can help reduce the risk of an incident controlling the organization rather than the other way about.

The first thing is to ensure that all information is flowing through the incident team. Certainly there will be actions taken by others, but they must be coordinated and under the direction of the incident team, which itself is at least initially driven by the continuity plan. Failure to grasp this coordination role will mean that the incident team is out of the loop and may be making decisions that conflict with events or actions that are occurring elsewhere – possibly even ones being made in their name.

The coordinator also needs to be wary of granting independent authority to others, outside their planned roles. This is not to say that he or she should fail to delegate but rather that they should be aware that delegation still entails responsibility for managing the delegated tasks.

The plan should have identified who, or what job title, is to assume the role of coordinator. This is so that everyone involved in the recovery knows who is ultimately responsible for it and to whom all issues should be raised. Clearly the recovery plan needs flexibility to allow for the nominated person to be absent at the time of the incident, but the plan processes should enable the information of who is in control to be filtered down to the others involved.

Consider the financial organization that, during a business continuity test, found that one person had been allotted eight different roles. Each one required him to be undertaking different tasks at various locations across the site.

Audit view

The audit challenge is to build into its review processes ways of ensuring that the incident team is always at the centre of events.

Most likely this will be achieved by developing a robust policy (see Appendix 7) that is communicated to all staff and consolidated by training and awareness exercises as necessary. This aspect also needs to be considered and observed during the testing phases of the plan (see Chapter 8). Finally, audit should review the parts played by all players to ensure that none has the autonomy to act in ways that could, actually or potentially, derail the smooth progression of the plan.

Audit should also ensure that the coordinator has the authority to make the decisions necessary for the recovery. This may be to invoke expenditure, stop business functions, redeploy recovery staff elsewhere or any other decisions necessary at the time and in the situation then pertaining. This authority may perhaps only be taken on in the event of an incident, but it may require the set-up of banking authorizations, credit cards and other matters that need to be undertaken before the plan is invoked.

Contain the incident

Once the nature of the incident is known and understood it is possible to start to contain it. By its nature of course this may have already happened. Fires, for example, tend to be tackled as soon as they are seen without waiting for authority to do so.

The situation may therefore take the form of:

- an incident that needs to be contained – e.g. a wall has blown down and unauthorized people can get access to organizational property and sensitive documents;
- an incident that has been contained but the aftermath has to be dealt with – e.g. a fire has successfully been tackled but there is structural damage as well as water and smoke still at the scene;
- an incident that appears to have been successfully contained – e.g. an attempted burglary was prevented;
- an incident involving an unknown situation – e.g. reports are coming in of storm damage in the region of an organizational warehouse, but solid information is not yet available.

For each of these types of issue there needs to be a proposed and recommended way of dealing with them. Usually this will be through the recovery plan using ideas, methods and approaches that have been drawn up beforehand and, ideally, tested. When this is not the case the coordinator will need to draw on experts to provide advice and assistance. Such experts may be external advisers and/or the emergency services as appropriate.

Containment approaches will obviously vary with the incident but the coordinator needs to have the authority and budget to invoke them.

Staff and others affected need to be advised as soon as it is practicable to do so. However, it should be borne in mind that no information at all creates fear, uncertainty and doubt in people's minds. It is therefore better to release regular reassuring bulletins to those involved than to leave it until a satisfactory outcome is certain, as that may never happen.

Ideally there should be a qualified team handling the people side of containment. This may include nurses, doctors and trauma counsellors where shock and injury are involved, but will certainly include press and public relations where communications with staff, stakeholders, and especially the media, are involved.

Audit view

Internal audit needs to be considering the implications of containment in the light of the risks faced by each business unit. In particular it needs to look at any specialist needs or long lead times that must be built into the plan in order to facilitate reasonable containment and recovery timescales.

Audit also ought to be looking at any special situations that may require particularly delicate handling. This might be where the organization is trading or involved in something that is perhaps not popular (e.g. animal testing) and where protests or attempts to exploit the incident may be made. In such cases the plan needs to recognize the increased risks following an incident and the need to contain those as well. It may be, for example, that the security services are alerted alongside the more traditional emergency services of fire and ambulance so that they can be on site to deal with potential issues.

Communicate with stakeholders

An organization involved in an incident needs to keep its stakeholders aware of what is happening and the realistic and likely recovery timescales and issues. This way they are more likely to respond positively and to work with the organization.

The recovery coordinator will therefore need to ensure that this is being undertaken and that those involved will be painting a realistic picture rather than an overly optimistic one that can never be fulfilled.

Staff who are not directly involved in the recovery process may have been sent home in the aftermath of the incident. They will be extremely vulnerable at this time to doomsayers and those that predict that the organization will never recover. It is in the aftermath of such an incident that many staff decide to quit the organization. It is important therefore that the recovery plan recognizes this sense of isolation and concern and provides positive and encouraging communication. A recovering organization cannot afford to lose many of its valuable staff.

Customers may not be able to trade and therefore need to understand what is happening in the short and long term. Some may even use it as an opportunity to try and avoid paying their bills. The organization therefore needs to provide reassurance that as far as possible it is business as usual. It needs to actively approach its known and largest customers with this message and to ensure that others are advised through the local and national media.

Invoicing may, however, need to be stepped up to improve cash flow in what may be an extended low-trading period.

Suppliers will also be concerned, possibly more so, as their livelihood may also be on the line. Again the organization needs to provide, as proactively as possible, a positive message. As soon as circumstances permit it should also provide alternative arrangements for goods and services and start undertaking payments to retain the goodwill of these suppliers.

Shareholders, especially the larger ones, may need a charm offensive to ensure that they remain involved and do not sell their shares, as this may trigger others to do so, possibly seriously affecting the market value of the organization. The relevant stock exchange would need to be notified if a publicly listed organization ceased trading or if serious difficulties affected its outlook or trading assumptions. There may even be a temporary suspension of trading in its shares.

Insurers and other advisers need to be involved for information and so that they can act in the organization's interests to minimize the cost and nature of the incident. Insurers may have requirements concerning how the organization recovers premises or other items (e.g. company vehicles) according to the nature of any policies in force.

Government agencies need to be kept in the loop to ensure that no regulatory or other issues are breached inadvertently or otherwise and to take advantage of any support that is available.

There may be considerable press and media interest and it should not be overlooked that the media could be on site very quickly after an incident. The use of social media and the rapidity with which information and images can spread through such media should also be factored in. As a result, relatives and friends of staff members may become aware of the incident almost before management has been able to begin the recovery processes. Additionally, with the nature of communications it may be that news of the incident is broadcast throughout the world. So managing the media interest and providing the best angle on the incident needs to be handled carefully and orchestrated by a dedicated press relations team. They may, however, need a spokesperson with the appropriate gravitas to deliver the message. No other staff should be allowed to talk to the media or to provide a view on the situation. This needs to be enshrined in the organization's policy statement to all staff.

In most cases the communications should be handled by specialist teams used to dealing with the various end clients. Although the coordinator will be involved and probably providing recommendations and advice, it may be top management that determines what is actually said to stakeholders.

Audit view

Communication is a very important aspect of the recovery process, as the nature and delivery of the message is crucial to how it is received. To a large extent this aspect happens after the plan has been reviewed by audit and can therefore only be analysed with hindsight after the incident has been dealt with.

As this is such an important area it may be too late to look back after the event. Audit should therefore consider seeking the development of some generic statements that the organization has available to use in the event of an incident. These statements may not form the actual statement at the time, but they would, at least, provide the right basis and convey the tone and sense of what needs to be said. These statements can be worked out with calm detachment and not in the heat of the moment.

The advantages of developing such statements ahead of time and including them in the plan include:

- they can be vetted by the organization's advisers;
- they cover the issues needed and will thus act as prompts;
- they will save time at a critical stage;
- they are available if the press or public relations team is not.

Audit should also ensure that anyone being used as a media spokesperson is comfortable in that role and has been suitably trained. In fact there may need to be at least one trained backup person available just in case.

One option that may be useful if available is a mass notification tool. This allows the organization to communicate with all those within a defined or geographic area.

Recovery of critical activities

Although this book has so far primarily looked at having one major plan with the option for other plans, it is at this stage that there might be a need for specific sub-plans for each of the critical activities. These sub-plans could either be alternative business continuity plans or a range of activity response plans designed to recover smaller activities or subsets of larger activities. There may also be a dedicated disaster recovery plan for the IT systems and services. The variety of options could also reflect the nature, risks and varying recovery needs of different business activities.

- An organization having identical retail shops trading in different locations would largely have the same plan, as each business unit would basically be the same.
- An organization that has three key business activities that are all different would need three completely different plans, for example a travel operator that runs shops in the UK, a charter airline and several hotels in Europe.
- An organization that has similar but different businesses might also require activity response plans, for example the travel agent with retail shops selling holidays but having in-store franchise outlets for currency exchange. Although these two operate from the same premises and therefore share similar problems, their recoveries beyond the basic bricks and mortar aspects would be very different.

The business impact analysis described in Chapter 4 would provide key input into determining the activities involved within the organization and their relevance and importance to business objectives. This will therefore form the basis of establishing the critical aspects.

Business functions can seldom be recovered in isolation and so the critical activities, which may on face value just relate to the business, may in fact go deeper. While a retail outlet could trade without any underlying technology by reverting to a cash box and ledger system, a sophisticated trading operation would continue to need power, telecommunications, equipment and data feeds. All of these would be critical activities that need to be recovered to ensure that the business unit can function.

These dependencies need therefore to be spelt out in the plan and identified in a logical sequence such that they can be recovered with the minimum of delay.

The recovery coordinator needs to have the necessary authority and budget to start the process. It is likely that there would then be a reliance on others from within and outside the organization to actually make things happen.

Audit view

Not surprisingly perhaps, given the importance of the recovery sequence, internal audit would need to be looking at the assumptions made and whether the critical activities were being recovered in the appropriate order. It is not unusual for this to be a matter of some debate, for example:

- Is it better to pay suppliers to keep them happy or claim money from customers to keep cash flow going?
- Is it better to restore the telephones before the electronic mail system? Which method of communication is better for customers, staff and suppliers?
- Should a retail operation revert to manual operation at the risk of higher fraud or await the recovery of its telecommunications and power to enable use of electronic tills? Can the electronic tills be opened or credit card readers be used without power? Similarly, could the outlet operate on a cash-only basis?

Ultimately it is management's responsibility to decide between the various competing options. Once the decision is made it should be enshrined in the recovery plan and not changed unless management authorize it. Changes may be necessary in the light of future business circumstances and this evolution of businesses is one reason why these plans have to be regularly reviewed and audited.

Recovery timescales

By developing a recovery plan the organization is acknowledging that it recognizes that there could be problems that it needs to overcome and that it is prepared to spend the time and effort to recover the business. It must, however, decide how much of the business to recover in the first hours, days, weeks and months of its recovery programme.

Much of this will have been looked at during the information gathering for the business impact analysis. In particular, the maximum tolerable period of disruption and recovery time objectives (see Chapter 5) will have been calculated for each business function.

To do this it must prioritize its business functions and its aims during the recovery period. The decision on what to recover is influenced by a number of factors, including:

- the impact on the organization of that part of the business being out of action;
- the type and nature of the incident and therefore the extent of the recovery;
- the time taken to recover and whether this can be achieved in stages to enable a phased recovery;
- the cost-effectiveness of recovery;
- the ability of the organization to fund a recovery.

From this it becomes clear what will be recovered and how much can be recovered in different time periods.

Recovery coordinators have the responsibility to initiate the recovery and they must either act as, or delegate the task of, project manager to ensure that the recovery is overseen and that the necessary activities are managed. Unless this happens the recovery will not proceed on schedule or in the order originally envisaged.

Given the importance of the recovery to the organization, top management need to keep close tabs on it. Depending upon its wider impact, the world media might also do so.

Audit view

The project team and management need to be challenged to justify the criteria used for the selection of which functions and how much of each function is recovered at the various recovery milestones of day one, two, three, and so on. This challenge should recognize that there is subjectivity in which units are recovered first but that there are certain essential business functions.

Organizations should not overlook the obvious in their recovery plans, such as site security and reception to protect the premises, assets and staff as well as dealing with enquiries. Marketing may not be needed immediately but public relations will be needed to deal with the media and stakeholders. That these thought processes have been followed should be obvious in the way the recovery plan is intended to be implemented.

Recovery levels

As part of the business impact analysis the various business units should have made clear the recovery levels needed for each of their activities. This of course would include the critical activities. The recovery team would have this information, as it has been refined into the plan, to guide them in their recovery endeavours.

The plan itself would then have been predicated on this information to give an indication of the recovery time objectives. These would also reflect what level of recovery is needed for each of the activities involved.

Some things can only be recovered fully. For example, electricity is either on or off. But business functions may not need to be fully operational in order to be able to start operating at a sufficient level to attract business. Shops can operate as long as they have stock, a salesperson and a way of taking and recording sales. The fact that they may not be fully fitted out is not necessarily a major consideration unless image is part of what the business trades on. It is this balance between what the customer expects and what the organization can give that determines what the recovery level is for each activity.

The recovery coordinator needs therefore to have the organization's visions and values firmly in mind in ensuring that the recovery aspects meet the need before they can be declared functional.

Audit view

Although internal audit needs to take a pragmatic view of the recovery process, it also needs to be aware of top management's vision for the organization and what aspects are most important. Failure to take that into account will lead to recommendations and suggestions that are not acceptable.

Before challenging any assumptions in this aspect therefore audit needs to review the objectives of the various business functions and the information contained in the business impact analysis documentation. This will provide a background against which assumptions and decisions can be reviewed.

Audit should also ensure that, where partial recovery is adopted, this does not create additional risks or hazards such as health and safety or data protection issues. Furthermore, it should ensure that partial recovery does not jeopardize any insurance claims or warranties that may be involved.

Recovery services

Organizations operate within a legislative and regulatory framework established by government and operated by public authorities that is designed to ensure the continued safety, security and prosperity of its citizens. When a large-scale incident occurs that threatens to disrupt significant numbers of people, such as a flood, public authorities are quick to act, first containing the damage and then rebuilding or repairing the damaged infrastructure.

Government and public authorities often have their own continuity or emergency plans. These could conflict with an organization's continuity plans, so it is important that liaison procedures are established and used to maximize coordination with public authorities. This is best undertaken in advance, while preparing plans to tackle any possible future incident.

Public authorities more frequently handle smaller-scale incidents. While an incident may initially affect a single organization, it might easily spread to affect neighbouring businesses and private residences if not promptly contained by the emergency services. Once an incident is contained, the affected area must also be made safe. Unfortunately for those engaged in business recovery, the authorities can often best guarantee public safety through exclusion until the area concerned can be properly assessed and hazards cleared. However, the public authority, unlike the affected organization, may have no urgent need to make safe or allow access to the affected area. In order to initiate salvage activities, restoration and repair work, the organization may need to work closely and cooperate with the public authorities.

Beyond the emergency services the organization will probably be reliant on specialists to restore various business aspects or functions. Some of these will come from within the organization, but others will be outside it. Wherever possible the organization should have established contractual or other arrangements with these outside bodies to ensure their fast response in the event of an incident. Failure to secure this may mean that the organization is unable to get professional help or support when required and this may delay or otherwise adversely affect the recovery timescale or the ability to recover all.

Audit view

The plan should identify the specialists that need to be involved in typical recovery options and how they can be contacted. This information should also include any special contact numbers or references that need to be used.

Particular staff may change or be unavailable. The list should also reference backup personnel and their contact details so that these can be called in as appropriate.

Recovery options

For the simple recovery from a power failure or loss of a file server organizations will cope without necessarily needing to evacuate the site, but for a major incident some form of external recovery facility is usually required.

The recovery facilities are not intended for long-term use and therefore need only support the essential first recovery options.

There are four main options:

Cold site

This is a site that could either be a data centre or an office location. It is equipped with basic accommodation needs such as air conditioning, electricity supply and communications. It will also have space to enable recovery equipment, supplies and materials to be installed as necessary.

As cold sites are the cheapest and most basic form of recovery provision, their power, communication and so on vary greatly. Organizations need to source equipment, software and supplies to equip them. This in itself can be a problem where lead times for deliveries may be in terms of days or weeks. Likewise, an organization will only be able to acquire state-of-the-art facilities, whereas their procedures, processes and practices may have been based on older generations of software or less powerful equipment for example.

Consequently cold sites take quite a time to set up properly and may not be appropriate for all types of organization. Furthermore, as they are incomplete they cannot be tested as separate entities.

Warm site

This is a site that could either be a data centre or an office location. It is equipped with basic accommodation needs such as air conditioning, electricity supply and communications. It will also have enough equipment already installed to enable backup support to be provided. Additional recovery equipment, supplies and materials will need to be installed as necessary.

Warm sites therefore represent a compromise between an unequipped cold site and a fully equipped hot site. They are far more customizable to an organization's needs and thus allow for items, such as those with a long lead time, to be purchased and set up but without incurring the full expense of having everything installed, ready and waiting.

A warm site may be only 50 per cent equipped to provide sufficient recovery facilities to get the business running again while the remainder of the equipment is brought in as and when needed. Equally it may be established within an area of the organization – such as a development facility – which is unlikely to be restored early on in the process and can therefore be 'sacrificed' temporarily to enable recovery to take place. This of course assumes the incident is not going to be the loss of this very building.

Hot site

This is a site that could either be a data centre or an office location. It is equipped with all accommodation and recovery needs. Only minor recovery equipment, supplies and materials will need to be installed.

Hot sites may vary in the type of facilities they offer, such as data processing, communication, or any other critical business functions needing duplication. The location and size of the hot site will be proportional to the equipment and resources needed.

As the ultimate disaster recovery solution, the hot site probably requires little more than a power switch to be turned on to turn it into a fully functioning business unit. Naturally they are costly and therefore suit only those organizations that cannot afford any kind of delay in getting the business recovered.

Mobile standby

Another option that is widely used is a mobile disaster recovery site. Essentially this is a vehicle that is fully equipped with recovery equipment that is driven to the site and used there.

It would normally only provide computing equipment and rely on local power supplies to keep it going. It is therefore more likely to be used in a disaster recovery incident than a business continuity one.

With the range of options available there is usually something to fit most budgets. The real problem, however, is for smaller organizations that are not capable of affording or financing one of these options. For the smaller organization the realities are probably as follows.

- Link up with a similar organization to set up a recovery plan. Each would then use part of the other's premises to effect their recovery. This can be a cost-effective approach but having another organization undertaking its recovery in your building may pose security and other difficulties. If it is adopted, however, it needs to be formalized in a contract.
- Managers could be responsible for storing key data and recovery information off site at their houses to provide an off-site recovery capability. Clearly there are security issues here that would need to be addressed and the organization would still need a recovery location, unless that is also planned to be in someone's house.
- Assume that serviced offices and other rentable spaces could be obtained at time of need. This may be a valid option unless the incident is a large one in which case many neighbouring businesses may also be planning the same option and thus taking up the available capacity. An up front contract for one of these units is probably not an option in view of the cost involved.

It is possible for an organization to have different recovery options for different business functions depending on their needs and criticality.

Audit view

Audit needs to review the recovery options chosen very closely to ensure they meet the needs and aspirations of the organization. In particular, they should ensure that the available facilities will provide recovery within the shortest recovery time period specified in the business continuity plan.

Audit should also be ensuring that the recovery facilities are conveniently located yet not so close that they may suffer the same incident.

Wherever possible the opportunity should be taken to test the recovery facilities to see what else may need to be provided to aid recovery and to ensure that they are a practical facility for the organization to use.

Where there are no recovery facilities provided audit should draw this to the attention of management. They will doubtless be aware of it but audit's role calls for it to raise the issue and formally ask management for an explanation of how it plans to manage the resultant risk.

Workarounds

While assumptions are being made about the nature of any risks facing the organization and the nature of their outcome, time may also be well spent looking at the sort of issues that the recovery team might face and developing some workarounds or fixes for these.

The most likely will be:

- lack of detailed incident information;
- lack of power or functionality;
- lack of documentation or key people;
- slower recovery than expected or clear-up, evacuation or other key aspects being delayed.

All of these will have an impact upon the recovery team and extend the length of the recovery project and the impact upon the organization, its customers, suppliers and workforce. It is therefore crucial that steps are taken to minimize the risk of these situations happening.

Audit view

The simplest technology is the one least likely to go wrong and therefore this should be the default option for everything related to the recovery team.

A specific internal audit review of the recovery team's role and their dependencies would prove a useful exercise. Under it audit could simulate the effects of various situations such as loss of power to the recovery team, missing paperwork and other aspects to see what backup functionality exists.

Such a review would have to take a pragmatic basis, as it is inevitable that criticism could be levelled at virtually every organization for some risk that could hit the recovery team. Nevertheless such a review could provide some useful pointers.

Clearly some risks should not even be accepted by the recovery team, such as being in the immediate location of the incident where they are actually at risk or taking unnecessary risks themselves.

Performance evaluation and monitoring

Whilst much of this project will have moved forward, with senior management being kept informed through their presence on the steering committee, it is at this stage that management will need to make decisions and commit further expenditure to this project.

The choice of recovery site provision, any necessary contracts for such services or fall-back arrangements that may be required just in case, will need to be made at a senior level. Top management may have delegated the authority or retained it but either way there should be a review of the project team's findings and conclusions before a final decision is made.

Audit view

If management want an in-depth review they may call on internal audit to undertake this; however, audit could pre-empt such a request and undertake this review ahead of any management request and offer their views to management as part of their overall consideration.

As has been noted before, the more information retained and documented, the easier and more comprehensive any review will be.

7

The continuity plans

Setting the scene

The theory side of the process is now complete and everything is in place for the organization to develop the all-important plans that will control its incident recovery processes. There are, however, still decisions to be made on what plans to build and what to include in them, as this chapter shows.

References

ISO 22301, clauses 8.4.4, 8.4.5.

PDCA model

This chapter forms part of the Check (monitor and review) phase of the business continuity life cycle.

Monitor and review performance against business continuity policy and objectives, report the results to management for review, and determine and authorize actions for remediation and improvement.

Introduction

Depending on the nature and requirements of each organization there may be any number of plans from one upwards. This would take into account the range of aspects to be recovered and the range of threats for which plans have been developed. It is, however, usual to have the following approach to this diversity of plans.

- Incident management plan – this is the top-level plan and is there for initiating any recovery and controlling how, and what, other plans are invoked.
- Business continuity plan – this is the main plan and, if there is only one plan, then this is it. In larger organizations, however, there may be multiple businesses or business functions to recover and so there could be a number of separate plans.
- Activity response plans – these deal with the lower-level recovery aspects such as air conditioning or water supplies and are likely to be sub-plans of a business continuity plan, but they may be stand-alone for smaller business functions.
- Disaster recovery plans – these deal with the IT function recoveries such as file, server and network losses. While they can handle all levels of incident, and will be used as such in organizations with an IT infrastructure but no business continuity plan, they would otherwise probably rank alongside activity response plans.

Where there are multiple plans or the plans can be invoked in slightly differing ways, for example where there are activity response plans or sub-plans for specific components, there needs to be clear indication how the various options should be selected and used.

An index to the plans, as shown in Table 14, Chapter 6, would serve this purpose and enable confidence in the option chosen according to the circumstances prevailing.

Despite the presence of the plan and an index, the recovery coordinator may need to use some discretion in the way the recovery or recoveries are organized. This would be because the particular circumstance involved is outside those envisaged when the plan was written.

If the incident is far outside the remit of the business continuity plan or activity response plan then these lesser plans may not be invoked, as the incident response initiative would remain with the incident management plan.

Audit view

Internal audit should be looking at the number of plans and ensuring that there is the absolute minimum in circulation. This is because there may be confusion at the time of an incident and it is possible that the wrong plan could be selected to be used. Similarly, the plans should be subject to change management and versioning to ensure that only the latest version is in circulation and that this is the copy that is available for the recovery coordinator and team to use.

Accepting that they might become cumbersome in some situations, it may perhaps be easier to have one plan with multiple sections that cover all the issues. In this the index and/or guidance at the end of each section would lead the coordinator onto the next logical task in the recovery.

Where multiple plans have to be used then perhaps colour coding, numbering or some other obvious tactic could be used to distinguish between them to reduce the risk of confusion at what will be a very stressful time.

Audit may be involved in any post-implementation review after the plan has been utilized. If this is the case, any use of discretion by the coordinator is going to be the subject of intense scrutiny, especially if it led to further problems. For this reason audit should insist that the continuity procedures require the coordinator to document the actions taken and the reasons. It might also be useful to require the time and date to be recorded for both decisions and key events, as this will help establish the timeline and sequence of events.

On the assumption that communications facilities are available after an incident it may be useful to hold an electronic copy of the plans and supporting documents to enable the incident and recovery teams to access the information quickly. It is likely that only wireless communication would be available after an incident and so the organization would need to ensure that the incident team had at least one wireless-enabled computer available if this approach is adopted. Alternatively, the electronic copies could be held on a USB flash drive or optical disk, although the latter may be slightly more prone to damage.

Where this data is held on any form of removable media, there are other issues to consider. The most obvious of these is ensuring that the data is up to date. This would require some kind of monitoring process to exchange or update media whenever changes in the base data were made. Security would also be important. The removable media would need to be protected against loss or theft and perhaps even against the holder overwriting it with other data. Additionally, where organizations have instituted lock downs to prevent removable media being used in their machines, there would clearly have to be a way for the recovery team to remove or by pass this restriction.

The incident management plan

The incident management plan is a self-contained document that sits above the business continuity plan. It should be the first port of call in the event of an incident.

Essentially it is a documented framework to enable an organization to manage any incident, whether or not the incident is covered by a business continuity plan. It may also be known as the crisis management plan, but the negative connotations of having a 'crisis' rather than an 'incident' tend to limit the number of organizations that refer to it that way.

Incidents outside the normal range of business continuity plans may include those that extend beyond the organization, such as terrorism or pandemics. They may also encompass the sort of incidents that organizations do not plan for, such as being taken over or experiencing a major fraud. In these cases it is likely that top or senior management, will direct the recovery operations itself without necessarily invoking the business continuity plan or the recovery team.

Audit view

The incident management plan is a key high-level document. Although it may simply be used as the first step towards employing a business continuity plan, it may also be used as a plan in its own right. For these reasons internal auditors need to be careful when reviewing it as its split role is likely to lead to the document being less detailed than audit would perhaps like for a plan, and also vague in its strategic recovery approaches.

Any review should therefore take into account that the plan is aimed at senior management and that this audience is likely to:

- make instant decisions;
- deploy budget and resources more easily;
- exploit the incident for other organizational gain or advantage;
- leave the detail to others.

A useful audit scope at this stage is to assess whether management is sufficiently prepared to deal with an emergency situation.

Establishing the plan

The key steps in establishing an incident management plan include:

- appointing a top management-level owner for the plan;
- defining the objectives and scope of the plan;
- developing and approving processes to build this plan.

It is likely that another project team will be established to undertake this task. It may, however, be part of the remit of the existing business continuity project team to ensure that the business continuity plan and the incident management plan are structured the same way and do not conflict.

The development structure for the incident management plan will be the same as that for the business continuity plan and will encompass:

- building the team to develop the incident management plan;
- determining the responsibilities of the members of this team;
- ensuring that this plan relates appropriately to other continuity plans;
- formulating the appropriate structure and content of the plan;
- determining the strategies to be embedded in the plan;
- gathering information and populating the plan;
- drafting the plan and consulting on its content;
- using feedback to update the plan;
- validating the plan – by testing if at all possible;
- obtaining sign off from top or senior management.

As the incident management plan is intended to steer the management through any incident, whether predicted or otherwise, its format is going to depend a great deal on the nature and complexity of the organization. It will probably take the form of a 'toolkit' in containing a set of resources that will be useful during an incident.

The plan may be developed on a modular basis enabling it to be updated easily and quickly. Different colours could be used to assist in finding particular contents more quickly. Regularly updated information, such as names and contact numbers, need to be kept in one section rather than throughout the text to reduce updating effort and the risk of missing something during an update.

Change control and version control management needs to be in place to ensure that the latest version of the plan is always easily distinguished from earlier ones and that updated copies are always available where the incident management personnel can access them.

Audit view

Developing the incident management plan could be undertaken as a separate exercise or as a spin-off from the business continuity plan, as much of the source information and analysis is common to both. Audit needs, however, to ensure that the business continuity plan is not delayed by the incident plan and takes priority.

Change and version control aspects need to be closely reviewed, as with the business continuity plan. It may be that as this document is intended for a more senior audience than the continuity plan, its security should be higher. This would certainly be the case if the incident plan discussed risk, fraud or business tolerance thresholds or other information that a competitor or attacker could use to compromise or exploit the organization.

Audit should also ensure that there actually is a plan and that top management are not simply expecting to manage any incident 'by the seat of their pants'.

Contents of the plan

Members of the incident management team should have specific roles and responsibilities during an incident. These roles and responsibilities should be defined in the plan. Any person without such a defined role should not be present unless specifically requested.

The sorts of tasks that will be required and for which someone should have responsibility include:

- communicating with emergency services, stakeholders and others;
- ensuring there are sufficient people in the incident and continuity recovery teams to undertake the tasks required;
- working with the recovery team to effect a managed recovery;
- approving expenditure as required. The recovery team is likely to have a certain delegated authority for spending, so this may only be for significant or unplanned items;

- managing the overall strategic impact of the incident and the direction of the recovery to ensure that any issues, concerns or opportunities that might arise are dealt with;
- maintaining a decision log throughout the incident.

The detailed activities associated with handling an incident are similar to those of the business continuity recovery plan. The main difference is that the incident management plan is likely to be less prescriptive, as the incident being dealt with will not have been predefined. Nevertheless, the incident management plan will need to cope with:

- staff and customers;
- welfare, counselling and evacuation;
- contacting emergency services and other support bodies or suppliers;
- moving people and materials both on and off site;
- communications with other services, as well as the media and other stakeholders.

Audit view

Internal audit will need to ensure that there are clear cut-offs in the incident plan when control should be handed over to the recovery team using the business continuity plan. Once that is done the senior management team or representative using the incident management plan is likely to have only a coordinating or communication role.

If, however, the incident team remains in charge of the incident then it must be responsible for its own decisions, with the recovery team taken out of the loop unless it is acting on the explicit orders of the incident team.

These matters need to be enshrined in the incident plan, and to some extent the continuity plan, to ensure that they are taken into account during the stress of a real incident.

Audit must ensure that the incident plan is written with no ambiguities that could be misinterpreted and no management speak or unexplained jargon that could lead to incorrect decisions being taken. The organization should also ensure that the plan is written in the appropriate language for those who will use it. This is particularly relevant where it is a multinational organization and one plan, or a similar plan, is being deployed across multiple countries.

A typical audit scope for reviewing the incident management plan may be to determine the adequacy and effectiveness of procedures developed for responding to and stabilizing the situation following an incident or event. The audit scope would also include the establishment of emergency command centres, invocation and composition of incident management teams and incident communications.

The business continuity plan

The purpose of a business continuity plan is to establish and document the way that the organization will respond to an incident. Those using the plan should be able to map the inputs they receive from the recovery teams against the documented responses in the plan and select the appropriate actions.

Situations outside the business continuity plan need to be escalated to top or senior management so that they can invoke the incident management plan.

The business continuity plan needs to be well set out and easy to reference, as it will be used at the time of an incident when there may be many other things and issues ongoing. The plan should therefore contain the minimum of extraneous matter and certainly not include any of the business impact analyses or other inputs that were used in its construction.

The development structure for the business continuity plan will be the same as that for the incident management plan and will encompass:

- building the team to develop the business continuity plan;
- determining the responsibilities of the members of this team;
- ensuring that this plan relates appropriately to any other continuity plans that the organization may have;
- formulating the appropriate structure and content of the plan;
- determining the strategies to be embedded in the plan;
- gathering information and populating the plan;
- drafting the plan and consulting on its content;
- using feedback to update the plan;
- validating the plan – by testing if possible;
- obtaining sign off from top or senior management.

Audit view

Bearing in mind that the plan needs to be very easy to use, audit should ensure that it has been designed on a practical or perhaps modular basis so that components can be updated as appropriate without, necessarily, the need to update the whole plan. Similarly, different colours could be used to highlight different sections or options, although this should not be overdone as it may make the document unpleasant to read.

Audit should check that regularly updated information, such as names and contact numbers, are kept in one section and not in the main text. This will reduce the amount of work required for updating and also the likelihood that not every incidence of a contact name or number is updated.

Change control and version control management processes need to be reviewed to ensure that the latest version of the plan is always easily distinguished from earlier ones and that updated copies are always available where recovery teams can access them.

Structure of plan

The plan is likely to include the following sections:

Administration or housekeeping section

This section covers the first part of the plan. It should include:

- title page;
- statement of purpose for the plan;
- indication of endorsement from top or senior management;
- security classification;
- distribution list and where copies are held;
- the plan owner;
- those responsible for maintaining the plan;
- references to related material, including external legislation and standards, internal policies, plans and guidance.

It is likely that this section would also include the current document version number and date along with a list of prior version numbers and the summary of the key changes made to each of those versions.

Contact telephone numbers and other details, such as reference numbers and activation codes to enable the recovery team to contact and invoke outsourced resources or services, should be grouped together so they can be updated easily. If individual's names were associated with a job role at this stage it would avoid having to use personal names throughout the remainder of the plan.

The administration section also needs to deal with how, when and by whom the business continuity plan can be invoked. In most cases this will be after an incident has been identified and the incident management team has decided that it can be handled through the business continuity plan (or plans) available. It may be, however, that the incident is recognized immediately as one that can be handled by the business continuity plan and management agree that the incident management plan need not be invoked. A further option arises when the incident has involved the loss of the incident management team members and so it cannot be invoked. In this case the business continuity team would have to undertake the recovery.

There should also be a list of the specific roles and responsibilities within the business continuity recovery team. Wherever possible the business continuity plan should use job roles rather than names as these will change less often. Each role or responsibility should have an individual associated with it and ideally there should also be at least one deputy for each key role holder.

Typical roles will include:

- recovery team coordination and management;
- initiation of key activities, such as evacuation;
- liaison with the emergency services;
- communication with on-the-spot response teams;
- communication with the incident management team;
- liaison with recovery services;
- liaison with the media – normally this would be the province of the incident team but may fall to the recovery team in certain circumstances;
- backup and support of other team members.

Critical functions

The next section of the plan needs to deal with the key business functions along with the impact upon them of specified risks and the recovery priorities and requirements. This is to provide the business continuity team with an understanding of the issues involved and the options and knowledge that they will need to aid the recovery process.

Recovery priorities and requirements for each critical business function can be developed based on the following information:

- the process for activating the response;
- details to manage the immediate consequences of the incident, especially welfare of individuals and prevention of further loss;
- the time frame in which the function must be resumed;
- the business and financial requirements for recovery of the business function;
- details of any external recovery arrangements to be invoked for the function;
- the staffing requirements for the recovery of the function;
- the technical requirements for the recovery of the function.

The next set of information needed is a business threat analysis. These are the potential incidents that the plan has been designed to deal with, along with the specific recovery steps for each. Not every incident will be the same and so this part will contain a range of different options, including the 'standard' ones of disease, fire, flood, computer virus, utility outage and terrorism.

This should be followed by consideration of the impact assessments that are used in the recovery plan. These will probably tend to take the form of the most wide-reaching option, as this approach would also cover the smaller incidents. For example, loss of a building would include all the elements of loss of power in one location, lack of access to the building, loss of customer records and so on.

For organizations that do not have dedicated cold, warm or hot sites, the recovery team preparations should include identifying two or three locations within each of the organization's premises, or a recovery room at an off-site location, where the recovery can be based. This avoids the need to find accommodation during the incident.

If possible the resources required for recovery should be assembled in advance and located in a dedicated off-site recovery room. For organizations with only one site or with restricted space on its sites this may not be an option. Where this is the case, the recovery team needs at least to identify what resources it requires and to store copies of these in locations that are less likely to suffer from any incident affecting the main location. These may include (subject to organizational security constraints) off-site premises of the organization's advisers (solicitors, accountants, etc.) or even the team members' homes.

These resources will include:

- the business continuity plan containing detailed recovery procedures;
- up-to-date contact lists (which should be in the continuity plan);
- staff lists for the location involved;
- heat, light and power;
- communications equipment;
- office equipment such as desks, chairs, stationery and, possibly, computers;
- cash or credit cards (plus bank account details);
- headed stationery and company papers;
- stock lists (if appropriate);
- first aid equipment;
- information relating to the business operations involved, such as customer lists;
- contracts relevant to the location;
- insurance policies;
- documentation relating to recovery services, emergency services, utilities, etc;
- IT hardware and software inventory lists;
- service-level agreements;
- recovery checklists;
- outline plans of how to stand down after the incident.

Some of these items may be in the battle box discussed later in this chapter.

Recovery

The business continuity document should contain (or provide links to) a range of information that will enable the recovery teams, whether they are internal or external, to commence the recovery phase as soon as possible. These recovery teams could include emergency services, telecommunications, utilities, building services and many others according to the nature of the incident.

For a typical recovery team the information required will include:

- designated assembly areas for each location where staff and others can assemble away from risk and threat;
- the nature of accommodation and work space available to use and to house restored services and workers;
- the contact individuals involved, ways of communicating with them and their responsibilities;

- location of technical infrastructure, such as telecommunications, power and water, as these could affect recovery approaches;
- any workarounds that are being used or planned;
- the maximum period that functions can be unavailable;
- peripheral requirements such as stationery and furniture.

It is likely that the business continuity plan will also identify the most cost-effective recovery solutions that are available for each business function based on the nature of the incident encountered. These will probably be based on a combination of recovering the minimum functionality required to perform and using the minimum time frame available to do so. These solutions will then be used as guidance towards achieving the recovery.

Audit view

Developing a business continuity plan in a structured way is essential, as dealing with an incident is a stressful time and information must be easily available or it will be missed. It is important that internal audit challenges the organization on the ease of use and simplicity of the documentation structure and format implemented. Indeed, this could well be an audit criterion to be assessed during testing of the plan.

The amount of information provided in the plan is also something that needs careful consideration. Although there is a risk of overloading the recovery time with information, there is also the concern that the business continuity plan may, because of the incident, be the only place where critical information about a business function is to be found. Likewise, during the recovery phase, suppliers and others may seek information about a function that will assist them, such as technical questions on IT systems that the recovery team would not be able to answer without access to the specialist documentation.

The following audit scope ideas may be useful:

- determining whether the continuity plan is complete, clear and up to date;
- reviewing and assessing the business continuity plans in place;
- ensuring that adequate and effective contingency plans have been established to support the rapid recovery of the business in the event of an incident;
- ensuring that all the potential risks to the organization are identified and assessed in the preparation of the contingency plans;
- identifying concerns and issues and, where appropriate, making cost-effective recommendations for improvements that can be included within the plan;

- assessing and reviewing the planned restoration techniques;
- ensuring that the organization can recover in the time stated or in the time required if there is an applicable external timescale.

Activity response plans

Incorporating all recovery procedures into a single business continuity plan will soon produce a document that is too cumbersome and detailed to be useful. It may be appropriate for larger organizations, who are the ones most likely to have multiple recovery plans, to separate these recovery plans out as individual activity response plans.

Activity response plans may therefore exist to support the recovery of discrete parts of the organization, such as the loss of all IT systems, or a part function within the organization, such as recovering the electricity supply or the air conditioning. The complexity and urgency of the aspect or function involved may mean that even more detailed procedures, plans and supporting documentation have to be available. In this context there may be a need for wiring diagrams, ventilation shaft plans and so on.

These plans will be developed after the business continuity plan has been established in principle and will be as a result of the need to keep that plan manageable and also to separate out the more detailed recovery aspects. In view of this, the activity response plans may be largely produced by staff within the appropriate business functions.

To achieve this, the functions will need to:

- appoint a person who will be responsible for each of the activity response plans and who will liaise with the business continuity plan project team;
- define the objectives and scope of each activity response plan;
- develop a timetable for completion of these plans with priority given to the specific business functions that need to be restored in the fastest time;
- work with the business continuity project team to ensure the activity response plans mesh with the business continuity plan;
- work with the business continuity project team and other activity response plan project leaders to identify and establish, as far as possible, a common standard layout or template for all activity response plans;
- consult widely on the draft plan to bring in a range of views;
- update the activity response plan in the light of feedback;
- validate the plan through testing;

- deposit copies of the activity response plan, and any subsequent updates, with the business continuity project team;
- ensure that the plans are included in the change and version control management systems used by the business continuity plan.

Development of the plans will generally follow a similar methodology to the business continuity plans with interviews, risk assessments and observations.

Audit view

Although these plans will be more the responsibility of the business functions, nevertheless they need to conform to the principles, objectives and stringent controls of their larger brother, the business continuity plan. Internal audit needs to ensure that this is the case.

The activity response plans should still be invoked through the incident management process and their place in that process is shown in Table 13, Chapter 6.

Disaster recovery plans

Disaster recovery is the process of recovering IT systems and services. It is perhaps more established than business continuity in that it is an essential part of computer-based systems that provision is made for loss or failure.

Much of what has been discussed under business contingency planning is relevant to disaster recovery. The following issues are as important to disaster recovery as they are to business continuity planning:

- management commitment to the disaster recovery process in terms of providing appropriate resources;
- the identification of requirements and the planning and implementation of standby arrangements, including the need and use of hot, warm and cold or mobile recovery sites;
- testing of the disaster recovery arrangements and the need to report on the results and make changes to the plan as appropriate;
- the need to update the plan in the light of changing systems, people, responsibilities and external events.

While these plans will have been developed by IT staff for IT staff they will nevertheless tend to conform with the principles and patterns of the other continuity plans because they are all concerned with recovery from an incident.

As long as they remain independent plans invoked through the business continuity plan there is no real need for them to be changed. If, however, they are intended to be meshed into the business continuity plan and not remain stand-alone they may need some rewriting to remove jargon and simplify or explain technical issues.

Developing the plan

The key considerations that should be taken into account in producing a disaster recovery plan are as follows.

Identification of risks

Risk assessment covers all of the IT systems, including data, networks and critical systems. Consideration also needs to be given to allowing non-affected systems to continue when others are non-operational.

Identification of critical IT

A fully detailed impact analysis needs to be performed to identify which of the organization's IT systems and infrastructure are the most business-critical.

Recovery

IT restoration plans should include all IT systems and networks and incorporate testing for functionality after recovery.

Providers

There should be more than one supplier for key IT services and the organization should verify third-party suppliers' disaster recovery capability.

Network resilience

Networks should be designed to be fully redundant with no single points of failure.

IT resilience

No critical system should depend on a single person for recovery or be installed in a single location.

Data

All critical data should be copied or replicated at another site.

Security

IT security is based on a number of individual elements, such as firewalls, encryption, anti-virus products, patch management and controlled data access and storage.

Site

The IT centre should be a separately maintained environment with access control and its own power supply, plus backups, air conditioning, ventilation and fire and water detection.

Alternative site

A backup site should be available to recover IT services.

Review, audit and changes

All changes should go through an agreed and signed-off procedure. The criticality of IT systems should be reviewed regularly.

Testing

IT recovery tests are required to realistically reflect incidents. The worst case scenario where all critical systems must be restored concurrently is the ultimate test. Critical systems recovery should be tested regularly.

Audit view

Because of the nature of the disaster recovery plans it is probably necessary for audit to use experienced IT auditors in the review. This is to ensure that technical issues are fully appreciated and not misunderstood.

Such a review would ideally be undertaken by a cross-functional audit team using both IT auditors and generalist auditors who would be more familiar with the principles and practices of reviewing the organization's business continuity material.

One aspect that is particularly important is to have an up-to-date inventory of the organization's hardware and software. This information can be very useful in negotiating with suppliers for new equipment as, particularly with the software, it indicates that the organization already holds the licences for use of the software and should not be required to pay the full costs of replacements.

The inventory lists will also serve as a blueprint for the kind of IT architecture used, if needed, and as an indicator to the insurance companies of the nature and size of potential loss.

A further aspect to consider is the need to understand what communication links exist and where dependencies and risks lie across the network.

Consider the organization that regularly tested its disaster recovery processes, including full recovery. During these tests it had never actually shut down the main system. When an incident did occur that shut down the main system it was found that the servers at the recovery site did not work. It was later discovered that these servers communicated with, and depended upon, some key software that was held on the main system.

Some ideas for audit scopes that may be useful include:

- reviewing and assessing the disaster recovery plans in place;
- ensuring the optimum contingency arrangements are selected and cost-effectively provided;

- ensuring that an authorized and documented disaster recovery plan is created, kept up to date and securely stored;
- providing the means to promptly and accurately recover from system failure or incident;
- ensuring that the organization's data is adequately protected from loss, damage or compromise;
- visiting and conducting fieldwork at the backup disaster recovery site to assess physical and logical partitioning controls;
- reviewing the recovery arrangements for any outsourced data such as that held in remote locations (e.g. cloud-based systems).

Invoking the continuity process

People need to understand how to react to an incident. The more often that procedures are practised, the more likely people are to react in the most appropriate manner for the real thing.

While most companies will have fire evacuation procedures as part of their health and safety requirements, many will not have well publicized instructions in place for responding to other events such as telephone bomb threats, leakage of hazardous materials, flooding or the receipt of suspicious packages.

Any incident procedure must conform to the requirements of public authorities or emergency services, and avoid any unnecessary risks. Incident procedures also need to define actions beyond the immediate response. Business recovery starts as soon as an incident occurs.

Audit view

Customer-facing and other staff at the front line, including telephonists, reception and call centre teams, need to be aware of the process for reporting an incident as they are the most likely to receive advance warning of a deliberate threat or to hear from a passing member of the public.

The business continuity training and awareness programmes within the organization need to focus on the importance of any messages of this nature being received and passed on accurately to a specified central point. The training needs to cover all staff but focus specifically on customer-facing ones to emphasize their role in this process.

Out-of-hours contact is more likely to be to a nominated person or number, or to a senior member of the organization, all of whom should be aware of the nature of the recovery team and how it can be contacted.

Consider the owners of a 15-storey city-centre office block. Several of their clients were likely targets for attack so they decided to test the alert and evacuation processes. They did this by hiding a red suitcase (to simulate a bomb) in one of the offices and waiting for it to be found.

Sequence of actions

The organization needs to define how the business continuity process is invoked, how the process will work and who takes responsibility for the various decisions that need to be made.

The likely sequence of actions will be:

- incident detected and reported;
- report passes to the person responsible for making a decision;
- assessment of the incident and its impact;
- decision on whether to invoke the continuity plan.

There is no guarantee that the person identifying the incident will be aware of the reporting structure. They may be someone outside the organization or it may be an automatic alarm or trip system that alerts a person some distance away from the site.

Once the incident is noticed, knowledge of its existence will be passed to the organization. This may or may not be immediate. It is possible that the involvement of the organization is not appreciated at first or that no contact for them can be found quickly. It may be that the emergency services have been contacted first and are already dealing with the incident.

The process of advising the organization is not always going to be easy and the contact chosen in the organization may not be involved in the continuity recovery team, but may need to contact someone else. Clearly this whole process can take some time.

Consider the organization that suffered an incident. When it invoked the incident management process it was found that all the key players had left their copies of the business continuity plans at home 'as they would be safer there'.

Once the incident management recovery team is involved they can begin to assess the nature and impact of the incident with a view to determining whether any of the continuity plans need to be invoked and, if so, to what extent.

Consider the organization whose incident management team each had their own copies of the plan. One person had an out-of-date copy and when an incident did take place he went to the wrong recovery location.

The likely first thoughts of the recovery team once they know about the incident might be as follows.

- Is this an incident and, if so, what are the issues?
- What is the timescale – how urgent is this?
- Where are the business continuity plans?
- Who else is on our incident management team, and how quickly can they assemble?
- Who else inside our business needs to be notified immediately?
- Who could be affected, internally and externally?
- Is the media likely to be involved?

Factors that will influence the decision to invoke the recovery plan (fully or partially) could include the availability of staff, the accessibility and usability of work areas, availability of resources and systems, and for how long any of these are likely to be unavailable.

An incident needs to be managed at every level, from ensuring the well-being of employees and the public, to managing the public, customer and shareholder perceptions of the incident. The manner in which a message is presented can affect the viability of a business, as many companies have found to their cost. This responsibility falls to a team of senior managers, normally including members of top management.

Audit view

Responding to incidents may not be a quick process, especially if the incident happens out of hours or on a public holiday. However, prompt recovery can often mitigate some of the problems or at least enable recovery action to take place more quickly.

Internal audit should therefore ensure that the organization has taken reasonable steps to minimize the time delay in getting the recovery team involved or at least aware of incidents. This can be achieved through ensuring that all likely organizational contact points including switchboards, senior management, branch offices and so on have up-to-date details of who should be contacted. Similarly the emergency services should also have this information. It may be that the organization provides a standard emergency contact number in all documentation and publicity that is switched through to the appropriate responsible person as required.

Decisions and procedures

If the incident is one that has been predefined in a business continuity plan then this should be invoked and the recovery team assembled immediately. If not then the incident management team, likely to be made up of senior managers, needs to be brought in.

If an incident management team does have to assemble, it will probably follow a set of procedures as follows:

- open a log in which to record all decisions and events;
- set incoming telephone lines and brief switchboard operators;
- brief any local incident management contacts and appoint a recovery coordinator;
- agree objectives;
- establish an incident management team room;
- gather as much information as possible;
- alert outside advisers if necessary, including trauma counsellors if the situation is stressful;
- agree which audiences need to be informed, both internal and external;
- agree and define messages for these audiences and prepare statements;
- think through likely questions and answers to reduce response times in stressful situations.

Perhaps the most important consideration for any organization embarking on an incident management plan is that it can only succeed as a top-down initiative, with top management owning the process.

Audit view

Internal audit should review the incident management plan to ensure that it meets its objectives and any assumptions are appropriate given the information known at the time of its preparation.

It should also be checked to ensure that it deals with the practical aspects of getting others involved and starting the actual recovery.

One point that has to be considered in this multicultural world is to ensure that those chosen to lead and be involved in the recovery team should speak a common language well enough to be understood and get their message across in times of stress and confusion.

Battle box

A 'battle box' is the name given to a secure box containing a variety of equipment selected to assist with the management and control of a business continuity incident. It needs to contain the key things that a team will require when invoking the recovery procedures. It therefore needs to hold copies of the continuity plans and any related documents. It is likely to also hold other items; what these are will depend upon the incidents that had been anticipated, for example, for damage assessment after a fire or an explosion or essential business items to support a business unit at an off-site location.

Typical items that might be considered for the battle box include:

Essentials:

- up-to-date copy of the business continuity plan;
- key management and staff contact details;
- copies of any contracts relevant to recovery (people, equipment, processes, etc.);
- building site plan plus spare keys;
- software and hardware inventory;
- insurance documents;
- financial information such as bank details, cheque book, credit cards;
- key stationery including that for logging expenditure during the incident;
- first aid kit;
- hard hat;
- two-way radios and batteries where the organization uses them.

Useful items:

- torch and megaphone plus spare batteries;
- disposable camera with flash;
- a charged-up mobile phone and a landline handset for backup;
- dust and toxic fume masks;

- water and food;
- tool kit including insulated equipment and gloves.

Apart from its content, the other major decision with battle boxes is where to locate them. This is relatively easy for large organizations where the boxes can be held at each location. For smaller organizations, this may well not be practicable and they may need to look at other options. Some of these may include locating them near the front entrance, at a secure off-site location, in the cars or at the homes of top management.

The other point to consider is whether there will be total reliance on a physical battle box at all. Some organizations ensure that all continuity plans and other documents are held securely in electronic format. The theory is that they can then be recovered at any location using wireless technology or they can be downloaded from a USB flash drive or other media. Clearly, this can only cover part of the equipment that may be needed in an incident but it does have some value (and risks) in certain circumstances.

Audit view

Battle boxes are a popular item and are available commercially containing the basic items that may be necessary. They are also of value for those below the management level and some of the items (hard hats, first aid kits and torches for example) may be more suited to those on the ground who are undertaking the recovery rather than those directing it from afar.

Finding a suitable location for a battle box can be a problem as, by its very nature, it contains things that others may want. Handing the box out to staff or leaving it under the desk at reception is very likely to lead to it being either unusable, or of limited value, should an incident occur. If it is to be located in an open area then there need to be regular checks to ensure that the contents are kept up to date.

Another issue is that if the battle box contains recovery plans and information that is of great value to an attacker. There clearly need to be security processes in place to protect the data over and above any physical assets. Internal audit should be ensuring that such checking is in place.

Where this information is held electronically, the security issues remain but also the concern as to whether wireless access will be available. If the incident is widespread this may not be the case. Similarly, not all locations have good wireless access, which may restrict access and download speeds. In looking at this aspect, internal audit also needs to consider whether an incident might generate so much mobile phone traffic that the networks become virtually unusable.

Taking the decision

In many cases the decision to proceed with the recovery process will be determined by the nature of the incident being within those already considered and anticipated. If the plan has been predicated on, say, a bomb threat or a fire, then these types of incidents would be easier to deal with. Where the incident is a variance on an expected threat, say a lightning strike that takes out all power, then any plan dealing with a total power loss would be suitable to at least start the recovery process.

Where, however, the incident is outside the normal and expected range, such as subsidence from mines not shown on local records or unusual and extreme weather, then the decision will have to be made locally by the incident management team coordinator on the strength of the information available, including an assessment of any damage involved.

Audit view

Internal audit should ensure that suitable guidance is available to the incident management team coordinator to ensure that they understand what assumptions are built into the likely recovery situations and the margin for error or variance.

Audit may also wish to reinforce the incident data gathering approach highlighted in Table 12, Chapter 6.

Beyond this, audit needs to ensure that there are suggested recovery processes and priorities for the most likely threats and risks and that these are clearly laid down, perhaps in an index to the plan or as part of the incident management plan to ensure that the coordinator can find and follow them at what will be a difficult time. Where there are alternative, but less likely, options it may be that these should be documented or at least discussed briefly so that the coordinator is as well informed as possible.

Who should be involved?

When an incident is declared the nature of that incident will identify some of the players who need to be involved. The emergency services, for example, will handle injury, evacuation and primary containment. The organization's own staff will contribute to this and perhaps handle some of the logistical issues such as maintaining contact and assessing preliminary organizational and business damage.

The coordinator will need to be aware of the situation as it unfolds and ensure that a senior management representative is briefed so that appropriate decisions can be taken quickly and effectively.

Depending on the nature of the organization there may be a need to involve advisers on the specific nature of the incident. A shipwreck for example will require different advisers to a mining accident or railway derailment.

Legal advisers may be called in where the incident puts people or property at risk or potentially has created some other form of liability.

The coordinator may also need to deploy staff and others in order to understand, mitigate or manage the incident.

Other organizational advisers may be needed such as marketing, public relations and human resources. These may be required to deal with staff and other stakeholders.

In general, staff will respond to an incident and provide such help as they can give. The coordinator and the emergency services will need to be sure that in providing such support, staff and others are not put under an increased risk, or are performing tasks for which they are not properly equipped or trained.

Certain facilities will be required for any recovery and these may have been provided up front in anticipation of their value. Items like fire extinguishers, for instance, will be available to be used. Most other equipment, especially if it is large or expensive, will not be provided in advance but would have to be called in as needed. If this kind of recovery is anticipated then it is possible that contracts or other arrangements would have been put in place to be invoked as part of the recovery plan.

Audit view

These contacts should be documented in the plan and it is one of audit's responsibilities to ensure that there is a process in place to keep this list as up to date as possible.

Similarly audit should review the list of advisers to determine if it is appropriate and current given the nature of the organization and the risks and threats identified against it.

Being able to use staff and others to deal with issues may be immediately helpful but will not be a long-term solution. The plan will therefore need to be reviewed to establish what has been put in place for medium- and long-term support and what steps the coordinator needs to take to invoke this support.

The plan should also be reviewed to ensure that it contains some references to health and safety obligations so that the incident coordinator can ensure that staff and others are not taking, or put under, any unnecessary risks.

Communication

Communication with others is one of the key issues related to an incident. It is essential that the organization keeps staff, the public and stakeholders aware of what is happening, although the degree of detail provided and the way the messages are framed may be different for each audience. Part of this may also be the need to maintain neutrality in the messages especially if there is a risk that the organization may subsequently be held responsible for the incident.

It is for these reasons that professional staff well used to presenting this kind of information should be used. The messages should be endorsed by top or senior management before release, but the messages themselves should be crafted by media professionals. One or more senior management member may need to be used to provide the necessary gravitas in facing the media, but the nature of their responses may be laid down by others.

Consider the organization that, realizing the risk that their chief executive officer was always the spokesperson for them, arranged for all the other senior management to individually present a set of typical business recovery statements to a panel of professional public relations people. Their style and approach were assessed and they were then given individual coaching.

Audit view

Audit should ensure that the processes are in place to provide a professional and slick media operation. This may require the preparation of outline press releases for inclusion in the plan to save time in the event of an incident. It should also ensure that members of senior management are coached in the ways to present themselves and their messages when speaking to the media.

Post-implementation review

When all the work has been completed and the plans are finally in place, it is time to consider what has been achieved.

This is the traditional time for audit to conduct a post-implementation review. This is a regular part of the audit landscape and is a way to ensure that the time and effort spent on a project has been worthwhile and determine whether the project has delivered what was expected of it. Even where a project has not fully delivered, a post-implementation review is useful to help determine what went wrong, why, and how things can be improved next time.

Although much of this work could, and should, have been undertaken through the life of the project, there is still an opportunity to look at the subject as a whole and to pick up issues or aspects that may have been missed due to other priorities or constraints.

Essentially audit should be looking at the criteria established for the project, which, at its most basic, was the project brief (see Chapter 2). Primarily this is to ensure that the project delivered what was expected and planned for by top management. There may have been changes on the way and these, together with the way that the business continuity management framework (see Chapter 3) have been implemented and developed, would also form part of the review brief.

The project papers will identify all the assets and risks unearthed as part of the close look at the organization (see Chapter 4) and these need to be reviewed to ensure the issues identified have been raised and carried forward. This is essential, as otherwise the recovery strategies developed (see Chapter 5) will not be correctly focused.

Vetting the theoretical recovery processes (see Chapter 6) and the plans (see this chapter) as far as is possible needs to be undertaken but, to a large extent, this cannot be verified until true testing has been carried out (see Chapter 8).

Nevertheless, some attempts should be made using desk testing or other passive testing or validation processes.

The review should also look at the plans themselves and whether they are easy to use, comprehensive and relevant to the organization. Ensuring that they are part of a robust change control process but protected within the organization's security processes would also be appropriate. Table 15 contains a checklist to test a plan's effectiveness. There may of course be more than one plan to consider.

Table 15 Plan effectiveness checklist

Question	Yes	No
Does the organization have a clearly defined, up-to-date business continuity plan covering its risks, weak links, mission-critical activities and their dependencies?		
Does the plan reflect the most up-to-date business impact analysis and risk analysis?		
Has the plan been approved and signed off?		
Is it clear who is responsible for the plan's maintenance?		
Is the plan regularly reviewed?		
Does the plan establish a clearly defined response to an incident?		
Does the plan clearly define how to recover critical activities within the specified time frame?		
Does the plan clearly define personnel roles, their accountability, responsibility and authority?		
Does the plan contain clear aims and objectives?		
Is the plan easy to use?		
Does the plan contain details of the business continuity recovery roles and responsibilities?		
Does the plan clearly state the appropriate responses according to the emergency?		

Clearly any 'no' boxes ticked should be of great concern at this stage.

An overall view of the effectiveness of the project can thus be formed and an audit opinion reached on the state of preparedness that the organization has achieved. Top management should be made aware of the findings of this investigation, as should the project manager. Any recommendations for change or improvement would then be considered within the ambit of the business continuity management update process. If accepted, they would feed into the future versions of the plan and thus complete the plan-do-check-act life cycle.

Performance evaluation and monitoring

The various plans are really the final culmination of the project and document the way forward for the organization if there is an incident. Although they will have been vetted and reviewed by internal audit and senior management along the way, they will not be subject to the real rigours until they are actually tested.

The monitoring processes will therefore be looking at how well the plans match the criteria and whether they appear to have the correct provisions for the various issues such as the recovery, getting services up and running and the welfare of staff and others.

Another aspect that needs review at this stage is to ensure that there are detailed provisions and processes to help the organization stand down from the incident. This will generally be through a gradual recovery of the various business functions and a winding down of the incident and recovery team roles. However, there may be some noticeable impact upon the organization if the incident was very serious and the recovered business functions are not as extensive as they were originally.

Audit view

Internal audit may well have undertaken a post-implementation review by this stage and have views on the project that they have taken up with management. If this review provides a positive assurance then management will, in all probability, be quite satisfied.

Audit, however, need to maintain their focus on this project as until all the plans are tested there can be no guarantee that they will work as expected. Similarly, audit needs to start looking at the winding down phase approaches to ensure that this aspect has been given sufficient consideration.

8

Exercising and maintaining the continuity plans

Setting the scene

With the plans made and in place the organization may want to take a breather. This, however, is not a good idea, as the plans need not just to be in place but also proven to work. As this chapter explains, testing the plans encompasses another range of issues, including keeping the plans up to date to cope with new risks and future business changes.

References

ISO 22301, clause 8.5.

PDCA model

This chapter forms part of the Act (maintain and improve) phase of the business continuity life cycle.

Maintain and improve the business continuity management system by taking corrective action, based on the results of management review and reappraising the scope of the business continuity management system and business continuity policy and objectives.

Introduction

It is essential to test that the business continuity plan or plans actually work. A great deal of time and effort will have been invested in producing them and before they should be relied upon they should be tested to confirm that at least the primary assumptions are correct. This is especially true when the plans have been developed by people outside the organization.

There are a variety of ways of testing the plans, from those that cause little inconvenience, but equally test very little, to those that involve the whole organization in a huge upheaval, but enable it to learn a lot about its plans. Organizations have the choice of how they approach this aspect, but clearly the more proactive their approach, the more likely the plans will be known to work if an incident should occur.

Ideally, each organization needs to conduct exercises and tests that:

- are consistent with the scope and objectives of the business continuity management systems (BCMS);
- are based on appropriate scenarios that are well planned with clearly defined aims and objectives;
- taken together over time, validate the whole of the business continuity arrangements and involve all the relevant interested parties;
- minimize the risk of disruption of operations;
- produce formal post-exercise reports that contain recommendations and actions to implement improvements;
- are reviewed to ensure continual improvement;
- are conducted at planned intervals and when there are significant changes within the organization or to the environment in which it operates.

Exercising the plan

Testing can be carried out across the whole plan, but this is disruptive and until the plan has been at least partially tested, it may be unwise to attempt a full recovery. The damage to the organization in implementing an untried recovery process may be significant.

Desk checking the plan should occur before it is published to ensure that the basic ideas are correct. However, it is not unusual for this checking to be carried out by those who have drawn up the plan and therefore have preconceived notions and assumptions. This can be mitigated to some extent by engaging an independent person to be involved in the exercise. Testing, however, should ideally be carried out beyond this and by those who are likely to have to implement the plan rather than those who drew it up.

As part of its testing process, the organization may wish to draw up a schedule to ensure that all parts of the plan are tested on a regular basis, although not all at once.

Some testing may never take place. The idea of deliberately halting a commercial production process or other key activity just to see if it can be transported to another location and made to work there, is rather a daunting prospect and is not to be carried out lightly. The idea of the testing is not, after all, to create more risks for the organization but rather to find ways to reduce or mitigate them.

Table 16 provides an overview of the different types of testing that are traditionally carried out and what is involved at each stage.

Table 16 Plan testing options

Exercise	*Description and objectives*
Desk check	The simplest form of test. This is a non-invasive process that usually only involves the project team that developed the plan and an independent person, perhaps a manager from another business function. It is conducted by reading through the plan and its aim is to ensure that the plan is not out of date and appears relevant. The primary objectives are to ensure that: • roles and responsibilities are accurate; • internal and external contact numbers are current; • content is reasonable.
Walk-through	This is a non-invasive process that only involves the project team that developed the plan and the recovery team that is likely to implement it. It is conducted by going through the plan in detail. Its aim is to ensure that those who will have to implement the plan are comfortable with its requirements and expectations.

Exercise	Description and objectives
	The primary objectives are to ensure that: • recovery team members understand their roles; • recovery team members understand the way the plan is structured; • the structure of the plan is reasonable.
Simulation or tabletop exercise	This is a fairly intensive process that involves the recovery team working together through a theoretical recovery exercise. As such it could simulate a full recovery or a partial one, such as IT services only. It is conducted by developing a realistic scenario against which the plan can be tested. The various recovery processes are followed in accordance with the plan. Its aim is to identify whether the plan actually works, and any improvements that could be made. The primary objectives are to ensure that: • recovery team members understand the importance of their roles and responsibilities; • problems identified during an incident can be solved by using the plan and involving the recovery team in developing solutions; • any weaknesses or gaps are identified and documented for later analysis and incorporation into the next version of the plan.
Communication testing	This tests only one component of the recovery process but may be quite an extensive test depending on the level of communication required and in particular the level of automation in the communication process. This latter may include mass notification tools that enable dissemination of information to finite geographical areas. Because of its nature it will involve the recovery team and other players, both internal and external. It is conducted by assuming an incident and then using the communication systems to inform and advise other players.

Exercise	Description and objectives
	The primary objectives are to ensure that: • contact information for key stakeholders is up to date; • the recovery team are proficient in the use of the communications tools and options available; • mass notification tools (if used) can be properly configured; • any communications weaknesses or problem areas are identified and reported on for later revision.
Recovery site testing	This is a significant test as it simulates an incident that closes one location and requires staff, IT, resources and services to relocate to the recovery site. It is facilitated by the recovery team but involves staff, service providers and the recovery location. The primary objectives are to ensure that: • the recovery site has the capability to allow operations to continue; • privacy, security and financial controls can be maintained during the recovery; • staff, and others, become familiar with the recovery processes; • IT and other services can be restored as needed at the recovery site; • employees and other workers can access the new site as required.
End-to-end testing	This is a full test of the plan. It goes beyond the recovery site test in that it includes trading partners, suppliers and others, as well as testing the connectivity between all the players. It is facilitated by the recovery team but involves staff, service providers and the recovery location along with trading partners, suppliers, emergency services and others, depending upon the incident simulated.

Exercise	Description and objectives
	The primary objectives are to ensure that: • the recovery plan works; • recovered processes and services are at a sufficient level to enable the business operation to continue functioning; • recovery levels are within expectations; • the various players, particularly the external ones, can work together to ensure the recovery works successfully.

These tests should be undertaken at regular intervals and the following frequency is suggested:

- **desk check** – at least annually;
- **walk-through** – annually;
- **simulation** – annually or twice a year;
- **communication** – annually or less;
- **recovery site** – annually or less;
- **end-to-end** – annually or less.

Audit view

Without a proper test there are no facts to support any belief either that the plans will work or that employees or critical third-party suppliers will know what to do in the event of an incident. Getting an organization to objectively restart its operations from its recovery address, in order to test the plan, is a non-trivial process that requires specialist expertise not always readily available.

Internal audit would therefore support any level of testing of the plan that is undertaken, but needs to be sure that the tests are carried out as part of an overall test plan and in an operational way, by people likely to have to shoulder the burden in the event of a real incident. In addition, the tests should:

- have one or more aims;
- be monitored;
- be documented for later analysis;
- lead to lessons being learnt and adopted.

While simulation exercises are time- and resource-consuming, they are the best method for validating a plan. Table 17 summarizes the key aspects to be incorporated into the exercise plans.

Table 17 Key aspects of a simulation exercise

Key aspect	Comments
Goal	Defines the aspects to be tested.
Objectives	The objectives for the testing should be drawn up using the SMART approach shown in Table 2, Chapter 2.
Scope	Identifies the functions or geographic area involved, along with the areas, aspects, considerations or assumptions to be tested.
Artificial aspects and assumptions	Defines how the test differs from reality by the use of artificial decisions and assumptions. Allows for variations and constraints to be applied to the test.
Participant instructions	Provides an outline of the tasks for the key players. The plans will provide the necessary detail.
Exercise narrative	Provides a background to the exercise. It will include discussion on how the incident was discovered, what it is, where it is and what has been done about it.
Communications for participants	To increase the realism emergency services could be involved and this would entail realistic communications. Management could also communicate changed assumptions during the test to create new test conditions.
Testing and post-exercise evaluation	Observers, probably including an audit team, will record the process of the test and any observations. Those involved will be keeping logs of events. There should be a debrief after the test to pool views and determine what worked and what didn't and also to recommend changes for the future.

The complexity level can also be enhanced simply by focusing the exercise on one part of the recovery plan rather than testing the whole plan.

Clearly internal audit is one of those best placed to report independently upon the tests and to be involved in the debriefings afterwards to determine whether the aims were achieved and whether the processes and actions undertaken were correct or otherwise.

Consider the financial organization that conducted regular simulation exercises. Its auditors insisted that every test had a random 'what-if' element where one or two of the recovery assumptions or dependencies were changed on the day to closer simulate reality.

No organization or individuals should feel threatened if the tests do not work correctly first time. This is almost to be expected as unanticipated events conspire to thwart the best-laid plans. Rain could slow down the movement of supplies, a door key or combination lock may not work, a critical player could be off sick. There are many events that might happen and the purpose of the tests is to determine how those events should be dealt with.

One aspect to be wary of is a particularly strong manager or individual affecting the way the tests are conducted.

Consider the fairly large organization that had a disaster recovery generator unit, the size of a container, installed near the IT building. To make the area more attractive a garden was built around it with paving, gravelled beds, flowers and trellis up the sides of the generator to accommodate climbing plants. Some time after installation a disaster recovery exercise took place and the generator was fired up. The hot exhaust pumping out killed several of the climbing plants. The organization's gardener complained directly to the chief executive and the test was stopped. No further disaster recovery tests using that generator were allowed.

This is not to say that they did not believe in continuity planning. During a subsequent drought the gardener, with the chief executive's support, arranged for a water tanker to come in every week so that the gardens could be watered.

Plans are often made and predicated on certain assumptions. After some time these assumptions may no longer be relevant or appropriate but the decisions having been made are not reviewed. Audit should be considering as part of this review how these ongoing issues can be managed.

Consider the organization that had its business continuity plans audited. The audit found that there were six people who could invoke the business continuity plan. At the time of the audit the situation was:

- *two were off sick;*
- *three had left the organization;*
- *the remaining person was on a six-month sabbatical.*

There may also be external contractual arrangements that have been entered into against assumptions made in the plan. Internal audit should be ensuring that these remain relevant.

Consider the organization that was paying an outsourcer a set fee to provide a recovery service. The audit discovered that the organization had not actually finalized its business continuity plan and so it could never invoke the plan or use the recovery service it was paying for. This issue had not shown up earlier, as the plan had never been tested.

Internally, audit may also want to review its own activities during the testing along the lines of Table 18.

Table 18 Internal audit activity review

Issues	Comments
What aspects of the business contingency plan were tested?	
In what ways did the plan succeed or fail?	
What was the internal audit involvement?	
Could the role of internal audit during this test be changed or improved?	

The following audit scopes may prove useful in assessing this aspect:

- ensuring that the continuity plan is tested at regular intervals and identifying whether lessons learnt in past tests have been addressed;
- attending and assessing the process for testing the disaster recovery plans;
- ensuring that the recovery plan is periodically tested for its relevance and effectiveness.

Exercising the operational systems

As part of the testing regime a variety of assumptions, decisions and extrapolations of the various operational aspects of the plan will be checked for validity. These will include the following specific components:

- technical activities and calculations;
- logistical processes and activities;
- administrative procedures and processes;
- procedural activities by business functions;
- any other operational considerations.

While desk checking will highlight a number of errors, it is only real testing that will unearth key aspects that have been overlooked. In some cases these will be simple things, such as not anticipating the need for a particular document, while for others it may be more serious, such as support vehicles being unable to find the location and therefore not being able to complete a recovery in the planned timescale.

Technical activities

These will include any technical aspects such as use of machinery or processes that require a more technical input or understanding.

Like other aspects, technical activities may have dependencies without which they will not function, such as power, fuel, maintenance, spare parts and so on.

Logistical activities

This will include the movement of items between locations as well as enabling staff, emergency services and others to reach the new site. It will also include recovering information, equipment and other items from the affected location, from off-site storage and other remote locations.

Administrative activities

These are the processes that underpin the workings of the plan. For example this aspect will include how each business function works and the understanding of the flow of information and/or materials.

Procedural activities

This covers the processes of each business function and its supporting dependencies. While the administrative aspects look at how the processes are managed, this part looks at how they work. Does that piece of paper always end up there in practice or are there variations? Does that job always take precedence over another job or is there another relationship?

Operational considerations

Operational considerations include other aspects or considerations that affect the running and performance of the business function or operation that the plan is designed to recover.

Audit view

Testing of these practical aspects of the plan is perhaps the easiest part of the testing regime and one that most people would be comfortable with. It is not so difficult to set the aims and objectives of the testing and to assess these criteria against the outcomes of the testing. Quite often it is a simple case of whether they work or not. Nevertheless, this testing aspect is complicated and presents many hurdles to a successful outcome. Not least is ensuring that things continue to work.

Internal audit should be keen to liaise closely with the business during these tests. It should act as an observer in addition to any documented role it may have in the actual recovery tests. It should use its observations, both from the independent viewpoint and from the operational perspective, to provide detailed and constructive feedback to the project team responsible for the tests. This team may be the original one charged with developing and writing the plan but may equally have been set up simply to conduct the testing.

In view of the differing nature of the operational aspects of the testing it may not be possible for audit to develop a comprehensive checklist of issues before the first tests, although it should have an outline idea of aspects to review. However, it should aim to develop a comprehensive list as the tests are conducted and evolve, as this will enable it to take not just an immediate view of the tests but also a longer-term view on how the organization is accepting and endorsing business continuity concepts and ideas. The longer-term aim for audit is to assess the way that business continuity has been embedded into the organization.

Any audit checklists and reports on the testing phase should be included with the documentation generated by others during the testing.

Exercising the arrangements and infrastructure

During the testing the ideas behind the plan will also be tested. This will demonstrate whether the thinking was robust, encompassed all the relevant issues and met the objective of the project, which was to develop a usable and appropriate business continuity plan.

Aspects of the plan that will be tested therefore include:

- continuity management arrangements;
- continuity management infrastructure, including:
  - roles;
  - responsibilities;
  - locations.

This will enable the organization to ensure that all the roles envisaged are necessary and that no more are required. Additionally it will demonstrate whether the level of decision making is as expected, as well as whether those holding the key positions are able to make appropriate decisions given the circumstances and information flow available.

Audit view

Internal audit also needs to be involved with this phase of the testing to ensure that the thinking behind the plan is appropriate. This includes the way the plan has been put together and the way it expresses information. If these aspects are not clear then the test will highlight them.

Audit therefore needs to develop criteria against which it can assess the robustness of the plan. Unlike the operational criteria, this checklist will probably be usable for all tests.

One of the key aspects that audit needs to consider is the security of information, data, personnel and the organization. During any test it is likely that the standards of control and management will be reduced. Audit needs to be aware of this and where it might put the organization at risk or compromise its activities and reputation.

Security may become a bigger issue in the tests if it proves impossible to complete a recovery in an anticipated time period due to unexpected problems, as that means that any planned safeguards may not be in place for the extra time that is involved.

Validating the recovery processes

The primary aim of the plan is to recover the business function or functions that have been subjected to the incident. It is therefore important that one of the outcomes of the testing exercise is to validate those aspects of the plan, including:

- recovery of the technology aspects and processes;
- recovery of telecommunications systems;
- availability and location of staff and others.

Technology is such an important part of most organization's operations that it is hard to divorce the technology from the operation. Most documents are produced and stored on computer systems, and many manufacturing processes are computer designed or controlled. Decisions are communicated via electronic mail. It is therefore in the nature of the recovery processes that technology plays such an important part.

So, too, do the telecommunications systems. Without the telephone links and connectivity that are taken for granted it is unlikely that the organization could communicate easily with its staff and stakeholders. It is virtually certain that the recovery team would be unable to manage a recovery unless they could coordinate matters using telecommunications systems.

The final parts of the jigsaw are the staff and others who may be necessary to make the recovery happen. These people need to be in the right place at the right time and must be able and allowed to perform the tasks that they have been assigned. In most cases the authority and access to continue will probably be given through the telecommunications and technology-based systems, while less often it will be directly from the coordinator.

The recovery processes need to ensure that these people are in the right place, at the right time and fully empowered to undertake the jobs for which they are there. A host of decisions, up front arrangements, logistics and other matters may need to be employed to get these people to that location, but once there they have to be effective.

Audit view

Internal audit needs to be aware of the requirements involved in getting the technology and telecommunications up and running and ensuring the right staff and other support are available and deployed appropriately. Audit should develop criteria for assessing these functions as well.

Audit may wish to probe the matter of staff not involved in these tests. Although they are not needed for this particular test, are they prepared if it is their business function that is affected by a real incident? Has management ensured that all staff are aware, or will become aware of the testing and what is involved, so that all are at least partially prepared for what they may have to do? Potentially some significant players from non-affected business functions could be involved as observers. Their role would be twofold: to act as independent observers of the test and to advise on any aspect of the recovery processes that would not work for their business activity.

Management should also consider communicating with all staff after the test to provide an overview of its successes. Naturally failures will not be highlighted widely but the mere fact of the test will bring home the reality of business continuity in ways that no memo, policy or management briefing ever can.

The matter of security is again paramount, as while staff and others should be given the access they need to perform recovery tasks, this should not be an uncontrolled or high-level access. They should still be given the minimum necessary to undertake their tasks and should ideally also be subject to standard organizational monitoring. This monitoring is designed to detect misuse of authority and errors so that they can be recovered from in the short term and prevented in the long term.

Essentially the recovery plan will be judged successful or otherwise on its results. It is, however, possible that a successful outcome may mask, or otherwise deflect attention, from earlier unsuccessful aspects that had to be 'got around' when they should have worked seamlessly with the rest of the plan. Audit needs to be aware of this kind of effect and to be independent and balanced in its assessment of the tests. There is no advantage to the organization to believe it has had a successful test if events occurred that may wreck the real thing if it ever happened.

Documentation

It quickly becomes apparent that the actual testing of the plan is only a part of the process. The other key factor is to record and document the nature of the test and its outcomes.

Getting the best from this aspect requires that criteria have been developed up front that the tests can be assessed against. While many of these will be the activities in the plan, there will be others such as identifying unexpected factors, recording delays, capturing staff workloads and so on that are material to the consideration of whether the recovery plan worked.

Each observer should be charged with the same role of recording their observations against the standard criteria, along with any other observations on other matters they feel are relevant. One useful insight mentioned earlier is that observers consider whether their business function could be recovered in this fashion. Some observers will have a more technical grasp of the issues and will therefore be better able to report some aspects than others.

The recovery teams should also be recording everything in an incident log. This should identify when actions were taken (including the time), why they were taken and what the outcome was. Any observations on the actions expected or taken should be noted.

All this material would then subsequently be used in a post-testing review to determine:

- what went right;
- what went wrong;
- lessons to be learnt.

Finally, the agreed results of this post-testing review would be documented and passed to the continuity management team to incorporate in the next version of the plans.

Audit view

As an observer, audit will also contribute to the documentation by completing the standard criteria. However, because of its specialist nature, it may pay particular attention to certain aspects such as risk, health and safety, security and information flows.

Audit should be involved in the post-testing review. Audit would not be running this as it is an operational matter. Nevertheless audit would still be able to contribute and discuss the issues that arose and help formulate any changes for the future.

There is nothing to stop audit conducting its own formal review of the testing and writing its own report to management. This would, however, need to be an approach agreed beforehand with management so that it was not seen as a way for audit to bypass or circumvent the operational post-testing review.

Reviews of the testing and lessons learnt should, of course, feed into the business continuity management process to ensure that they are passed forward into the next version of the plans.

Maintaining continuity management arrangements

Maintaining the plan is a vital process. Invariably organizations that have plans in place that have not been kept up to date, do have major problems in the immediate aftermath of an incident.

Maintaining the plan need not be a significant overhead, but it is important to have a regular review of the plan and its relevance to the organization and business functions. Typical review categories will include:

- **local changes** – including departmental growth, processes changing, staff arriving or leaving, staff training and awareness of continuity matters;
- **business changes** – including major shifts in the direction of the business, priorities, acquisitions, mergers and new markets;
- **testing** – inevitably there will be changes that can be made to the plan in the light of knowledge gained through testing;
- **audit/compliance** – many companies will change their business methodologies following audit and compliance reviews and recommendations;
- **implementation projects** – the process of implementing or revising a continuity plan or another business project may also suggest ways that lead to improving or refining the plan;
- **conformance** – ensuring that the organization continues to adhere to requirements, regulations, standards, guidelines and other aspects that impact upon its business functions.

As many people as possible should be involved in monitoring and commenting upon changes. Business continuity should become part of the culture of the organization, so that eventually all staff will recognize when changes are made that may have an impact on the plan.

In smaller organizations there may not need to be a formal review, but rather responsibility would be passed to local managers who would report changes that have occurred. These change reports could then be passed to those responsible for maintaining the business continuity plans for them to make the necessary changes or seek further information.

Audit view

Internal audit needs to be involved in the regular reviews of the plan with a view to ensuring the plan's continued importance within the organization. Audit should raise the issue if there are no reviews scheduled or if the reviews are put aside due to other pressures. It should also ensure that material generated from its own reviews, from tests of the plan and other sources, feeds through into the process to help inform the view and generate better plans for the future.

These regular reviews also provide an opportunity for the function responsible for managing the plan to check that the assumptions made are still relevant and that there are no new factors that need to be considered and integrated into the plan.

The remit of these reviews needs to be wide enough to consider not just internal factors but also external matters that may have an impact. Some of these factors may include business events or risks that are more likely to eventuate and perhaps to require the plan to be invoked. Where this is the case then the review team should be able to alert senior management of the situation with a view to undertaking mitigating or corrective action rather than a recovery after the event.

The review team needs to consult widely, including receiving input from all the business functions as well as from the infrastructure and support sides. Outsourcers and trading partners may also need to be involved. Clearly with all these interested parties a single meeting would not be appropriate, but it is likely that information gathering will take place year round and a scheduled meeting will take place regularly, such as quarterly, to hear recommendations and make decisions. Internal audit should be present at that meeting and contribute to the debate. Senior management should also be involved to ensure that the issues, including requirements for additional work, resources or funding, can be dealt with expeditiously.

Internal audit should bring matters of best practice to the table at these meetings to ensure that the organization is developing in accordance with its peers and to facilitate the incorporation of ideas and approaches.

If the organization is certified to ISO 22301 or equivalent, it should also be involving its external assessors in the outcome of these reviews to demonstrate progress and to ensure that the assessors have no concerns. The certification process, including these surveillance audits, is considered in Appendix 1.

In these reviews the organization may find that certain guidelines, regulations or other requirements are not being met. These non-conformities will need to be addressed to ensure that the organization does not suffer other consequences, such as legal action. They are also important as certification to the standard cannot be given or maintained if they exist.

A typical audit scope for reviewing plan maintenance and testing may include:

- assessing the adequacy and effectiveness of the processes for maintaining continuity capability;
- ensuring that the plan is aligned to the business and organizational strategic directions;
- assessing the plan's fitness for purpose and evaluating its assumptions based on any recovery or simulation test results.

Change control

Changes to any system or process should be controlled. This applies equally to business continuity plan processes as well as to any other system. A common cause of failure is inadequate control of changes to information, assumptions, decisions and approaches. Formal management responsibilities and procedures should be in place to ensure satisfactory control of all changes to the continuity plan and the processes that support it.

There also needs to be a formal process, or set of processes, in place to capture updated information from throughout the organization that could have an impact on the way that business continuity is structured. The likely inputs would include:

- results of audits related to business continuity matters;
- new or changing risks from business operations;

- new strategic directions;
- input from trading partners and suppliers;
- results of business continuity exercises and tests, including observers' notes and recommendations;
- improved recovery techniques, products or opportunities available from the market.

All changes proposed should be presented to a steering group who will vet the proposal based on information supplied and recommendations made. This steering group would, in effect, probably be the managers responsible for business continuity and key business operations. The recommended or essential changes should be accompanied by a justification for the change, business sign off if the relevant manager is not available and agreement of others who may be affected by the change.

If the change required is to an underlying technical system or process used by the business continuity team, say to improve data flow, then that change is also likely to have to go through the organization's IT change control procedure.

Audit view

Formal change control procedures should be enforced. They should ensure that security and other control issues are not compromised and that management agreement and approval for any change is obtained.

Internal audit should be involved and should ensure that change control processes include:

- maintaining a record of any agreed authorization levels;
- ensuring changes are submitted by authorized users;
- reviewing controls and integrity procedures to ensure that they will not be compromised by the changes;
- identifying all systems and documentation that require amendment;
- obtaining formal approval for costs and resources before work commences;
- ensuring that implementation of the changes will not increase the risks or disrupt other business processes beyond the minimum necessary;
- ensuring that the plan and supporting documentation is updated on the completion of each change and that old documentation is archived or disposed of securely;
- maintaining version control for all documentation updates;

- maintaining an audit trail of all change requests and subsequent actions;
- ensuring that operating documentation and user procedures are changed as necessary to be appropriate for the new versions;
- ensuring that the implementation of changes takes place at the appropriate time and with due priority.

Despite having a formal and regular change control process, there may be particular changes or situations where the business needs to act quickly and cannot wait for a formal approval process to take place. The change control processes should recognize this and include a methodology for coping with emergency changes.

These should be controlled by a written process to ensure that they are justified, are supported by senior management and can be incorporated without apparent further risk. They should still come before the formal process for retrospective approval and the necessary updating of documentation and procedures as appropriate in due course.

Performance evaluation and monitoring

In many ways, the tests are the time for evaluating the progress of the project – if the tests show everything works then the project has been a success. Or has it? The tests show that the project has built plans that can be tested successfully but they do not show that the organization can be recovered. Nothing but a full-scale incident can confirm that and that is precisely what everyone has been trying to avoid.

What management needs to do to properly evaluate the project is to ensure that the tests and conditions are as realistic as possible, that assumptions are kept to the minimum and to ensure that random elements – things that are not covered in the plans – are introduced to ensure flexibility and to generate creative thinking.

This is another aspect that needs to be considered – that the incident and recovery teams must be guided by the plans but are capable of thinking rationally and logically to find acceptable solutions when the plans are insufficient or the circumstances do not match the assumptions in the plans.

Apart from the performance of the project teams, management should also be monitoring the other players to ensure that their roles are carried out properly and that they contribute to any lessons that need to be learnt as a result of the testing. These aspects will feed into the processes of bringing business continuity into the organization's culture.

Audit view

Wherever possible, internal audit should be involved in any business continuity testing, providing the testing team with impartial, experienced observers.

Audit can use the tests both to feed into the project and also to update their understanding of how the processes might work in practice. Both of these roles then help audit to feed in a better level of assurance to management.

9

Bringing business continuity into the culture

Setting the scene

The business continuity management framework is in place along with the plans, but so far this knowledge has been restricted to a relatively small number of people in the organization. Now is the time to spread the word widely and to ensure that every employee and contractor is aware of their business continuity responsibilities and, furthermore, they carry them out.

References

ISO 22301, clauses 7.3, 7.4.

PDCA model

This chapter forms part of the Act (maintain and improve) phase of the business continuity life cycle.

Maintain and improve the business continuity management system by taking corrective action, based on the results of management review and reappraising the scope of the business continuity management system and business continuity policy and objectives.

Introduction

Having invested a considerable sum in terms of resources, time and money into developing a business continuity plan, it is unreasonable to just leave that plan on the shelf awaiting an incident.

The plan is a living, breathing document that needs to be managed and maintained in order to ensure that it can perform properly if it is called upon after an incident. This nurturing process will not bring full dividends until the concept of business continuity is embedded into the organization's culture and both staff and management understand and work with it.

Realization of the importance of business continuity usually comes with the recovery of the business after an incident. That is when it really penetrates people's minds and they realize its importance and value. Clearly no organization wants to have an incident just to raise awareness and other ways must be found.

Audit view

Internal audit should be supporting and pressing management in its efforts to raise the profile of business continuity, as it satisfies one of the key roles of audit: that of having appropriate processes in place to deal with risk. Internal audit is charged with providing assurance to management on the risks faced by the organization and what better mitigation strategy for some of those risks than a fully functioning and tested business continuity process?

Another way of integrating business continuity ideas and objectives into the organization is to develop metrics or key performance indicators that staff and managers are assessed on and that relate, in this instance, to business continuity. These could include the following indicators.

- The change control process supports and includes the business continuity plan policy objectives.
- The continuity policy is included in the metrics for performance and compensation for all staff levels.
- Each task in the continuity and recovery plan is assigned to a specific individual. On a regular basis the individual is required to certify that:
  - they are aware of their assigned responsibility;
  - the task procedures work as documented.

- Specific metrics and penalties are included in all service-level agreements and contracts.
- The status of the continuity plan is a regular agenda item for all executive, middle management and team meetings.
- Business continuity is incorporated into the business process development and operational procedures.
- Business continuity plans are required and verified for key suppliers and customers.
- Service-level agreements that support continuity planning objectives are implemented with key customers.

Any metrics used for compliance must be clearly defined, implemented across all staff and measured in a clear and consistent way.

A useful audit scope may be to confirm that key personnel are aware of the existence and the content of the plan.

Leadership

Business continuity is an initiative that can only emanate from the top of the organization. Although staff might see the need for business continuity, it will not happen without senior management support and leadership.

The same is true for any plans or processes to embed business continuity into the organizational culture. These plans therefore do not just need to be endorsed from the top, but rather senior management should be seen to be endorsing, promoting and abiding by them. In this way the plans acquire credibility and importance.

Audit view

There are many examples of failed attempts at bringing in change through a 'bottom-up' approach. This is where newcomers to the organization are trained in ways of doing things that existing staff and managers do not know, use or understand. Not surprisingly the new ways do not last as the new recruits are encouraged by their managers and peers to use 'established' methods. The new ways then fall into disuse.

It is therefore essential that business continuity should be introduced top-downwards and, as one of the advisers to senior management, audit should be supporting this approach.

Assignment of responsibilities

Once top management has agreed and promulgated the need for business continuity to become part of business thinking, it needs to assign the responsibility to achieve this to a person or function. Achieving top management's vision may require several functions or teams to work together to make things happen.

Throughout the process there should be clear responsibility lines and clear role delegation.

Audit view

Internal audit may not necessarily conduct an audit of this part of the process, but will undoubtedly come across the evidence of this approach in other audits. It will then be able to vet the appropriateness of the approaches taken, the resources and costs involved and the advantages and benefits gained.

Measuring benefits and assessing advantages and disadvantages is a difficult exercise and requires clear and straightforward criteria to be developed and used consistently across all functions and activities. It is often ideal to develop these before the need is identified rather than have to put something together in a hurry.

Awareness

The most likely ways of raising awareness of business continuity across an organization will include:

- posting items on noticeboards and bulletin boards;
- dedicated pages on the intranet and/or staff magazine;
- promulgation of a business continuity policy for all staff to adhere to;
- information circulars, internal newsletters and management briefings;
- agenda items on team discussions;

- inclusion of business continuity in all organizational projects;
- sending staff on training courses;
- including business continuity responsibilities in job profiles;
- endorsement of, and certification to, ISO 22301.

The real aim of all or any of these approaches is to bring the subject of business continuity to the attention of all staff and to explain to them what it is and what it does. Having outlined this, the role of business continuity within the organization needs to be discussed. From there it is a logical step to the role of the individual within business continuity within the organization.

One way to generate a buzz about business continuity is to publicize it and make it big news in your organization. Maybe a business continuity fair? A one-day event to draw in staff across the organization, show them the effects of incidents, show them what the organization is doing, quiz them on how it could improve matters, entertain them and get them involved and thinking. Publicize it in an in-house newsletter and promote your organization's caring credentials in the local schools and press.

A smaller organization may not wish or be able to afford to go down that route but perhaps here an electronic mail to all staff to raise awareness and coffee break discussions to bring up the issues involved could be effective. Once started, the awareness ball rolls on and all publicity is good publicity.

There may also be a need to raise the awareness of business continuity within trading partners and other third parties where interdependencies exist between them. This will ensure that all are aware of the issues and how they affect each other.

The ultimate purpose of the exercise is to make each individual a component of the business continuity process. Each staff member should be made responsible for reporting anything that may have an impact upon business continuity. This will include:

- reporting to a designated person any incident or potential incident that could have an impact upon business or support functions;
- identifying to local management any system or other changes in business functions that could have an impact upon the business continuity processes;
- identifying to local management any changes or proposals that may improve business continuity processes or activities.

Ideally the responsibility of reporting any incidents or potential incidents will be enshrined in an organizational business continuity policy. Such a policy and how it can be developed and audited is discussed in Appendix 7.

Audit view

Members of staff need to be involved in the process, or see the value of their input, before they will take any responsibility for it. The processes identified as ways of raising awareness need therefore to focus on these aspects as well as raising more general awareness of what business continuity is and what it involves.

Internal audit should therefore review or consider awareness-raising material in the light of the value it brings. This may mean that to assess the value of such exercises it needs to seek the views of the audience rather than the presenters. This moves the focus of audit downwards and stops the exercise being purely one relating to the quality and depth of the materials and media used.

A review of the business interdependencies should also be undertaken to determine whether trading partners and others should be involved in the organization's own awareness campaigns or should be undertaking such matters themselves. A review of the contracts in place would be needed to see if audit could undertake audit reviews of these other partners' awareness campaigns to check compatibility and mutual support.

Audit may also wish to consider a review of the effectiveness of the various methods of raising awareness. The feedback from such a review could considerably enhance the awareness programme and may lead to more cost-effective methodologies being used.

Raising and maintaining awareness is not a one-off event, but needs to happen regularly. Partly this is to remind staff of their obligations and responsibilities, but also to catch those new to the organization. Some of these new staff may have useful experience and ideas to contribute.

The following audit scope ideas will help test this aspect:

- ensuring that all internal and external parties to the recovery process are fully aware of their responsibilities and commitments;
- ensuring that users are made aware of their responsibilities with regard to the backup and protection of workstation data.

Training

An organization embracing business continuity should ensure that staff receive training in the skills they are required to develop, and are involved in business continuity at the level to which they have responsibility.

For the development project team manager and the development team itself there are some professional training courses on offer, along with professional qualifications. It would provide a great deal of additional credibility if the team manager, at least, was qualified. Apart from credibility there is also the not insignificant fact that the manager would know what they were doing and this would minimize mistakes and the undertaking of unnecessary activities.

It would also be useful for the project team to have training, or at least experience, in being involved in a project. This will include project management where appropriate as well as project methodologies. Where an organization uses one standard methodology for all projects then it will, in all probability, have a pool of skilled staff that can be deployed on any project.

It may be that the team manager and team members have been recruited from outside the organization because of their experience and knowledge in this sector or that the whole project has been outsourced. Where this is the case then the organization should consider requiring some form of skills transfer to be used to enable in-house staff to acquire at least the rudimentary skills if not to actually progress on to taking professional courses or qualifications.

For staff involved in the business functions there will need to be training to ensure that they are able to fully and effectively perform the roles they have been allotted. Much of this will be standard on-the-job training but there may also be an element of additional and specific training to cope with special or unique continuity needs. Specific needs may include:

- interviewing staff;
- conducting a business impact analysis;
- running a continuity exercise;
- risk and threat assessment;
- media communications.

Staff new to the organization should undertake some form of induction training. This is general training to equip them for working in the organization but it may need to include business continuity matters if there is an organizational policy on it and if management has deemed it to be of significant value.

Subsequent on-the-job training should then enable new employees to become more involved in their role within business continuity processes.

Staff training may be run in-house or may be outsourced according to the needs and aspirations of the organization. Where the training is conducted in-house using in-house staff they should have been fully briefed on the subject and be capable of presenting a cohesive and easily understood briefing on the subject. External training courses should also be vetted to ensure that they can provide the same or a better level of training.

Audit view

There is scope for internal audit to review training operations to provide assurance on staff awareness of issues that could have an impact upon the organization or business service. The critical assessment would be if the risk is increased by staff receiving no training or poor training.

Once business continuity training is in place audit may wish to carry out a training needs assessment to understand the levels of awareness of business continuity matters. Mapping this against management's expectation of the knowledge levels required will then highlight what further training is needed.

Audit would then need to validate its views of what further training should be included and how it should be implemented with a professional educational or trade body. This will identify what levels of competence and knowledge are required to deliver the additional training. The review of the training function and competence of the facilitators and trainers will then need to be assessed on their overall rated performance (from internal course assessments) and on perceptions of the audit team members when attending courses.

If no training is being requested or provided for business continuity or line staff then internal audit should draw this to the attention of senior management as an unnecessary increase in the risk profile of the organization.

A typical audit scope for reviewing training and awareness may be:

- determining the adequacy and effectiveness of business and organizational training programmes in creating an awareness of business continuity and the ability to execute relevant plans;
- considering the adequacy of the skill levels of professional business continuity managers at the business and organizational levels.

Training through testing

The processes involved in testing the plans are discussed in Chapter 8.

The value of a business continuity exercise cannot be overestimated as a way of informing staff and others about the principles and practices of continuity planning and recovery. It will highlight what can go wrong, how things can be recovered and what lessons need to be learnt as a result.

It is, however, an expensive way of teaching staff and needs to be used only as part of the regular testing plan to ensure that the business continuity plans remain workable and effective. Having said this there is no harm in bringing in additional staff as observers or spreading the net wider to get more people involved as a way of underscoring the awareness and training that they have already received.

Observers from trading partners, customers and other stakeholders may also need to be involved, as this may influence their own plans or reassure them that they can continue to rely on the organization because it has effective recovery plans in place.

Audit view

Although it is useful to bring in additional staff as part of their training there should be constraints on the numbers involved, as too many observers will hamper the recovery efforts. There is also the concern that these observers may even raise the risk profile of the event.

Audit may, however, wish to recommend alternatives such as filming recovery exercises to use as highly relevant training aids in management briefings and training courses. It may be useful to get the key players involved in these exercises to write articles for the staff magazine or items for the intranet so that a greater sense of interest and involvement is created.

Audit should also be aware of the security considerations of having those outside the organization present during tests and exercises. If necessary audit should work with appropriate functions within the organization to ensure that no data, trade secrets or other compromising information or activities are on view or available to those not authorized to see them.

Assessment

To determine how much value is being gained from the awareness and training exercises overall will require some form of management initiative to measure how the organization and its staff relate to business continuity. Perceptions of the change may go some way towards indicating whether awareness is higher, but only properly controlled polling and research will elicit reliable facts.

There is one issue to be taken into account and that is the basis against which the results of any survey are measured. Unless the organization undertook comparable research before introducing business continuity training and awareness it will not have a firm basis for showing how things have changed. It will have to assume that all knowledge has been gained from the training programme, which is not strictly correct.

Feedback should be encouraged from all training and awareness events. Criticism should be responded to and dealt with where it can be seen to be a consistent or significant issue.

Audit view

As this is not an operational matter, internal audit is well prepared to undertake some of this work and research, but may be better employed in reviewing others while they do it. This is to ensure that the other players, such as the training department, human resources and media, have ownership and accountability for the research. If audit undertakes it all then these others may dispute or distance themselves from the results.

Audit can, however, undertake its own research and this may highlight specific questions that need to be asked or issues that need to be raised in order to see the full picture.

Communication beyond the organization

As well as ensuring that there is appropriate communication within the organization about business continuity, management needs to establish and maintain communications with those outside the organization, and its immediate trading partners, who are also potentially or actually involved with any business continuity recovery. This will include:

- local community groups;
- the media;
- relevant authorities;
- any national threat advisory systems;
- emergency services.

Maintaining such communications may include attending meetings and responding to queries. It might also require undertaking presentations and sharing the organizational experiences with others. Such links and contacts may lead to the setting up of local and national support networks.

All of these activities will require the organization to provide some form of staff and other resources to support these activities. Such an investment may, however, pay dividends if the organization can receive earlier warning of problems, learns lessons from others' experiences or sets up communication channels that ensure faster or smoother recovery in the event of an incident.

The staff involved in this communication role are likely to be working with, or as part of, the business continuity team. This will give them confidence and up-to-date knowledge of their subject area, as well as recognizing significant and useful information that they can bring back from others in these groups. The closer they are to the business continuity team, the easier they can feed in any new information and this may help the organization in its ongoing continuity plan maintenance arrangements.

Audit view

Given the major expenditure and time invested in developing and maintaining the business continuity plans, setting up a team that both promotes the organization's achievements, and simultaneously captures information that could be valuable in keeping the organization one step ahead of any incidents, has to be seen as a benefit. For these reasons, audit should support these kinds of links.

With the skills these staff acquire, they would be able to run in-house training courses or write articles for in-house or external magazines or journals that concern business continuity planning. Their role could therefore partially overlap those in training and media functions and job rotation may be a useful way of defusing any potential problems with these other functions.

Such staff might also have job profiles and key performance indicators that measure the value they provide to the organization. This would help maintain the focus on continual improvement.

Performance evaluation and monitoring

With all the expenditure in money, time and resources that the organization has committed to the business continuity project, there should be a strong emphasis placed on ensuring that all staff and contractors are aware of their roles.

Management therefore needs to be looking at the ways that are being used to promote awareness, the level and type of training that is available and the ways staff and contractors are reacting to this. Passive introduction of a new policy and an offhanded approach to promoting awareness is not going to engender any enthusiasm or any likelihood that staff or contractors will be involved unless an incident actually occurs and it directly impacts upon them.

Ultimately, management have to believe in the benefits of business continuity and have to demonstrate this in their everyday decisions and actions. This enthusiasm will then cascade down through the organization.

Audit view

Internal audit have a dual role in this. They are observers of what the organization is doing and they are also employees of the organization. In the latter role, they will be aware of the steps that are being taken to promote business continuity and how these are being received by their colleagues in other functions across the organization.

This dual role provides audit with a unique way of assessing the initiatives and bringing it to management's attention without necessarily conducting a full-scale audit review. Given that audit is an impartial observer, management should welcome these views, as it gives them an opportunity to consolidate or change existing approaches, as appropriate.

Internal audit may wish to conduct a value for money audit on the various training and awareness-raising exercises that the organization carries out. This would determine the value and impact of each option compared to the cost involved. The findings from such an exercise would be very helpful to management in deciding where best to target their resources.

Appendix 1

Certification to ISO 22301

Specification

ISO 22301 provides a specification for use by internal and external parties, including certification bodies, to assess an organization's ability to meet regulatory, customer and the organization's own requirements.

Demonstration of successful implementation of the standard can therefore be used by an organization to assure interested parties that an appropriate business continuity management system is in place.

Certification process

The main auditing stages for gaining certification are likely to be:

Stage 1 audit

This is also known as the initial assessment or desktop review.

It covers the documented business continuity plans and the incident management plan to determine whether they meet the requirements of the standard.

Any outstanding matters will need to be addressed before the next stage can begin.

Stage 2 audit

This is also known as the conformance audit or certification audit.

This examines evidence that the implemented business continuity plans and the incident management plan conform to the organization's documented business continuity plans and incident management plan.

If any of the requirements of ISO 22301 have not been met, the organization will be required to agree to a corrective action plan to address the weaknesses. Once these issues have been addressed another conformance audit will be carried out.

Certification recommendation

Once the stage 2 audit has been successfully completed a recommendation will be made for certification. The audit report will be forwarded to the ISO 22301 certification manager for final review and subsequent issue of the certificate.

Surveillance audits

When the certificate has been granted, periodic monitoring of the business continuity management system, along with the business continuity and the incident management plans, begins. This process is designed to ensure that the organization's business continuity processes continue to conform to the requirements of ISO 22301.

Organizations certificated to other standards

There are a number of other business continuity standards to which organizations may be certificated. The main ones are:

- ASIS/BSI BCM.01:2010, *Business continuity management systems: Requirements with guidance for use*
- AS/NZS 5050:2010, *Business continuity — Managing disruption related risk*
- BS 25999-2:2007, *Business continuity management — Part 2: Specification*
- ISO/PAS 22399:2007, *Societal security — Guideline for incident preparedness and operational continuity management*
- SI 24001:2007, *Security and continuity management systems — Requirements and guidance for use*
- SS 540:2008, *Business continuity management (BCM)*

Organizations may choose to obtain certification under ISO 22301 either in addition to or in replacement of any existing certification.

Transition arrangements exist to enable organizations to move their certification seamlessly to another standard over a period of time, to reduce any unnecessary additional work. Usually the transition period will be up to three years but the exact time period allowed and any additional work necessary to achieve certification to ISO 22301 from an existing standard certification will need to be agreed between the organization and the external team that is providing the certification.

Appendix 2

Risk

The role of risk

Organizations of every kind face internal and external factors and influences that make it uncertain whether, when and the extent to which they will achieve or exceed their objectives. The effect this uncertainty has on the organization's objectives is 'risk'.

All activities of an organization involve risk. Organizations manage risk by anticipating, understanding and deciding whether to modify it. Throughout this process they communicate and consult with stakeholders and monitor and review the risk and the controls that are modifying the risk.

Definition

Risk can be defined as the possible variation in an outcome from what is expected to happen. Essentially it encompasses three aspects:

- **variability** – the future is not fixed;
- **expectation** – our vision of the future;
- **outcome** – what actually happens.

However, risk and uncertainty should not be confused, as they are not the same thing:

- risk is inherent in any situation;
- uncertainty arises only because we do not know all the facts.

While risk is normally taken to mean things that could go wrong, there is always the possibility that something could go better than expected. This kind of speculative risk, where things can go either way, is the basis of most trading.

With a great deal of data about the past there may be the ability to predict objectively what the risk of a certain event happening in the future might be, within stated limits of accuracy. But normally the historical data is incomplete or imperfect and the situation is not quite the same, so that it is difficult to be certain about the outcomes of an event.

Classifying risks

There are many ways of classifying risk and an appropriate classification can greatly help an organization in identifying and implementing its risk strategy.

Normally risks are classified according to their source or characteristics. A common distinction is between *business* and *non-business* risk.

Business risk

Business risks arise from the nature of the business, its operations and the conditions it operates in. They include:

- strategy risk – the risk of choosing the wrong business strategy;
- enterprise risk – the success or failure of a business operation and whether it should have been undertaken in the first place;
- product risk – the chance that customers will not buy the products or services in the expected quantities;
- economic risk – the effect of unexpected changing economic conditions;
- technology risk – the market or industry is affected by some change in production or delivery technology;
- property risk – the loss of property or losses arising from accidents.

Non-business risk

Non-business risk is any other type of risk, usually classified as financial risk, operational risk or event risk.

Financial risk arises from sources external to the business, including:

- liquidity risk – an unexpected shortage of cash;
- gearing risk – high borrowing in relation to the amount of shareholders' capital in the business, increasing the risk of volatility in earnings, and insolvency;

- default risk – creditors of the business failing to pay what they owe in full and on time;
- credit risk – the organization's credit rating being downgraded.

Operational risk refers to direct and indirect losses from failed or inadequate processes and systems, arising from both human error (internal operational risk) and external events.

Event risks arise from events that are mainly or completely outside the organization's control. These may include:

- disaster risk – an incident occurs, such as fire, flood, or death of key people;
- regulatory risk – new laws or regulations are introduced;
- reputation risk – the actions of the organization damage its reputation in the eyes of stakeholders;
- systemic risk – failure of a supplier or process to meet its contractual obligations, thus putting the system itself at risk.

Risk analysis frameworks

Another way of classifying risks is to use one of the recognized frameworks.

Auditors will be familiar with these approaches, but the following tables illustrate how these tools could be used to highlight some of the risks that a business continuity strategy may need to address.

PESTEL

There are a wide range of environmental influences that can affect organizational strategies and performance. The PESTEL methodology is useful for highlighting these and enabling analysts to capture a broad range of key drivers. In many cases it is the combination of the key drivers that affect the structure of an organization, sector or market. A PESTEL analysis table is shown in Table A.1. The key drivers will be those deemed appropriate for the organization; those shown are for illustration only.

Table A.1 Sample PESTEL analysis table

Influences	Key drivers for change
Political	• Government stability • Taxation policy • Foreign trade regulations • Social welfare policies
Economic	• Business cycles • Gross national product trends • Interest rates • Money supply • Inflation • Unemployment • Disposable income
Socio-cultural	• Population demographics • Income distribution • Social mobility • Lifestyle changes • Attitudes to work and leisure • Consumerism • Levels of education
Technological	• Government spending on research • Government and industry focus on technological effort • New discoveries and developments • Speed of technology transfer • Rates of obsolescence
Environmental	• Environmental protection laws • Waste disposal • Energy consumption
Legal	• Competition law • Employment law • Health and safety • Product safety • Data protection

The PESTEL framework may be used to determine risks at the present time as well as at any time in the future. It can therefore also be used to assist reviews of the resources required during recovery and the recovery time objectives (see Chapter 5).

Seven S's

Another framework exists for analysing the internal threats. Although this is not as well known as PESTEL, it is just as valuable and works in a similar way. It is known as the Seven S's and a sample version is shown in Table A.2.

An advantage of using the Seven S's approach is that it highlights issues that may become significant in a business continuity sense. One of these is the differences between empowered and bureaucratic structures. In the former, staff are encouraged to work on their own initiative and take actions that will benefit the organization rather than simply be told what to do and when to do it. In terms of business continuity, empowerment could mean that the organization is regularly being exposed to unknown risks and that recovery and other staff may not be where they should be, or involved in unrelated activities, when an incident strikes.

Table A.2 Sample Seven S's internal threats analysis

Influences	Key drivers for change
Strategy	• Centralized strategy across all business units • Top management holds control
Structure	• Hierarchical • Layers of management
Systems	• Standardized IT systems • Reliance on paper-based links to outside suppliers
Skills	• Training compulsory • Regular knowledge reviews
Staff	• Recruitment standards high • Low turnover rates
Style	• Low level of empowerment • Lack of creativity
Shared values	• Strong sense of ethics • Good organizational reputation

SWOT – Strengths, Weaknesses, Opportunities and Threats

The third approach is the SWOT analysis, which is used to summarize the key issues from the external and internal business environment. A SWOT analysis may simply be used as a collator for all the issues identified in the PESTEL and Seven S's analyses.

See Table A.3 for an example of a SWOT analysis.

Table A.3 Sample SWOT analysis table

Strengths	Opportunities
Flexible workforce	Contract with reliable recovery provider
Strong brand identity	Recovery plans integrated with suppliers
Simple and standardized IT structure	Ability to provide consultancy or benchmarking to others in the sector
Weaknesses	*Threats*
Lack of sufficient and up-to-date documentation	Protection of source materials is outside our control
Inadequately tested plan	Supply could be disrupted Prices could be raised
Plan not embedded in culture of organization	Surrounded by businesses whose incidents could affect us

While a SWOT analysis should help focus discussion on future choices and the extent to which the organization is capable of supporting these strategies, there are two potential drawbacks with using this approach.

- A SWOT exercise can generate very long lists of apparent strengths, weaknesses, opportunities and threats. It is therefore important to be clear about what is important and what is not.
- There is a danger of over-generalizing, which does little to explain the underlying reasons for that particular capability. There is still a need for rigorous and insightful analysis.

ISO 31000:2009

While all organizations manage risk to some degree, ISO 31000:2009 establishes a number of principles that need to be satisfied before risk management will be effective. It recommends that organizations should have a framework that integrates the process for managing risk into the organization's overall governance, strategy and planning, management, reporting processes, policies, values and culture. Such risk management can be applied across an entire organization, to its many areas and levels, as well as to specific functions, projects and activities.

Although the practice of risk management has been developed over time and within many sectors to meet diverse needs, the adoption of consistent processes within a comprehensive framework helps to ensure that risk is managed effectively, efficiently and coherently across an organization. The generic approach described in ISO 31000:2009 provides the principles and guidelines for managing any form of risk in a systematic, transparent and credible manner and within any scope and context.

The relationship between the principles for managing risk, the framework in which it occurs and the risk management process described in this Standard is shown in Figure A.1.

Organizations with existing risk management processes can use ISO 31000:2009 to critically review, align and improve their existing practices.

Identifying risks

The key tenet of any corporate governance system is that it is dynamic and not static. The organization, its working environment and the risks it faces are continually evolving and the systems of internal control have to be in place to ensure there are regular and thorough evaluations of the nature and extent of the risks faced.

Top management should lead the organization in identifying and evaluating risk. The process should be continual to catch new risks, reduce losses and identify risks that provide opportunities for the organization.

There are two main options when identifying and evaluating risks: a risk to earnings or a risk to assets.

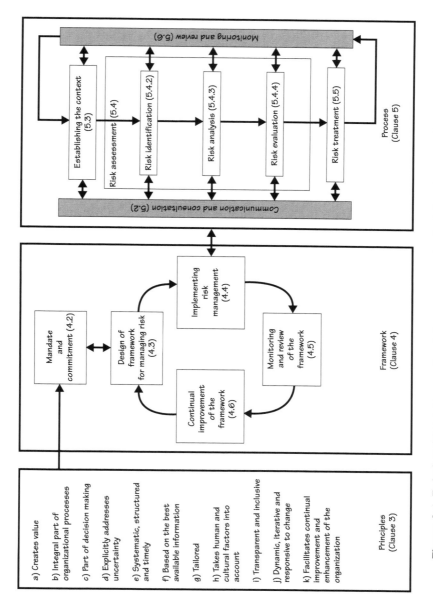

Figure A.1 Relationships between the risk management principles, framework and process

Risk identification involves reviewing the complete environment, both within the organization and outside it. For each risk environment and risk classification, there are potential pure and speculative risks.

In the strategy analysis process it is important to focus on risks that are specific to the organization, or the industry sector in which it operates, rather than general ones. They should be mapped to the relevant threats and opportunities that they represent to the organization. A plan for managing each specific risk can then be formulated.

Risk profile

Relating the risks to the organization's objectives puts the risks into perspective and enables actions to manage the risks to be prioritized and the significant ones dealt with first.

The risk analysis frameworks discussed earlier can be used to determine the risks, but the next stage is to develop a risk profile in relation to each risk. This can be achieved using a risk probability/impact matrix, such as that shown in Table A.4.

Table A.4 Risk probability/impact matrix

	Impact	
	Low	*High*
Probability *Low*	Risk 1	Risk 3
Probability *High*		Risk 2

As each risk is profiled to determine whether it is low or high probability (i.e. the chance of it happening is low or high) and its impact, it will fall into one of the four boxes in Table A.4.

Decisions can then be made on the basis of this assessment. The decisions are likely to fall into one of the four categories in Table A.5.

Table A.5 Probability/impact decision matrix

Risk profile	Strategy
High impact High probability	Take immediate action
High impact Low probability	Develop a contingency plan
Low impact High probability	Consider action to be taken
Low impact Low probability	Keep under review

To manage these risks the organization has to choose one or more of the following options:

- **terminate** – eliminate the risk by ceasing the activity involved;
- **tolerate** – accept the risk and work with it, although this may involve losses;
- **treat** – take steps to minimize the risk or its impact, perhaps through business process changes;
- **transfer** – move the risk to another party, e.g. by insuring against it or potentially outsourcing it;
- **take advantage of** – use the risk to gain some advantage, e.g. start up a new business function.

The choices made will be dictated by the risk attitude of the organization and its management.

Risk maturity and risk attitude

The organization's attitude to risk is dependent on its risk maturity, which in turn determines the approach to risks taken by top management in achieving corporate objectives. The five levels of risk maturity are:

- **risk naive** – no formal approach has been developed for risk management (lowest level of maturity);
- **risk aware** – scattered 'silo' based approach to risk management (everyone doing their own thing);
- **risk defined** – strategy and policies are in place and communicated; risk appetite is defined but risk register is possibly incomplete;

- **risk managed** – enterprise approach to risk management is developed and communicated;
- **risk enabled** – risk management and internal controls are fully embedded into the operations (highest level of maturity).

These approaches to risk reflect the outlook of management, with risk naive organizations being more likely to take risks because they do not understand their risk exposures.

Because some aims and strategies are riskier than others, the attitudes of management towards risk can be implied from a combination of:

- the leadership from top management;
- the organization's objectives;
- the strategies being considered to achieve the objectives.

Primarily there are three attitudes that determine this:

- a risk-averse attitude would opt for the lower risk offerings;
- a risk-neutral attitude would opt for the best expected return, regardless of risk;
- a risk-seeking attitude would opt for the highest anticipated return, even if the risks were also higher.

Top management should ensure that the risk appetite is communicated to stakeholders.

When it comes to evaluating strategic options, management's aim may not necessarily be to avoid or reduce risk, but to build a balanced portfolio of risks that are within the limits of the organization's risk appetite and that support its aims and strategies. In practice there are likely to be different levels of risk appetite for different operations or individual businesses, and a portfolio view of risk and return will be taken.

Aggregating risk

Controlling and managing the risks in the organization is a complicated matter because:

- there are likely to be different risk appetites in different parts of the organization;
- there are likely to be different risk appetites in respect of different risks;

- risk must be aggregated across the organization when designing corporate and business strategies to meet objectives;
- the organization needs to balance its portfolio of risks;
- the organization needs to communicate its overall risk portfolio to stakeholders.

Thus all the risks must be aggregated on a 'risk map' or overall risk profile, so the organization, and its management, can see the nature of all the major risks that it faces.

Risk assessment

Risk assessment means evaluating:

- the severity of the impact of a possible outcome;
- the likelihood of that outcome occurring;
- judging whether the risk is acceptable to the organization.

Very often risk assessment involves judgement only, based on qualitative information. In such cases the evaluation can simply be 'high', 'medium' or 'low'. Risk assessment can be backed up, if required, by quantitative data that assigns values and probabilities to outcomes, so that overall the risk has an expected outcome expressed as a number.

Appendix 3

Auditing the business continuity life cycle

Systems life cycle

Almost irrespective of the project itself and where the support, management and expertise comes from, it is necessary for an organization to ensure that basic development rules are established and maintained for all projects, whatever their size and complexity. This ensures that they are properly planned, built to perform the tasks required and can be run. Running or testing the implemented project then provides feedback that can be used to improve the project.

The basic steps in the systems development life cycle used for business continuity are defined by ISO 22301 as:

Plan (Establish)

Establish business continuity policy, objectives, targets, controls, processes and procedures relevant to improving business continuity in order to deliver results that align with the organization's overall policies and objectives.

Do (*Implement and operate*)

Implement and operate the business continuity policy, controls, processes and procedures.

Check (*Monitor and review*)

Monitor and review performance against business continuity policy and objectives, report the results to management for review, and determine and authorize actions for remediation and improvement.

Act (*Maintain and improve*)

Maintain and improve the business continuity management system by taking corrective action, based on the results of management review and reappraising the scope of the business continuity management system and business continuity policy and objectives.

As the 'act' phase contributes feedback into the 'plan' phase for any changes, revisions or replacement systems that may follow, the life cycle is circular and sustainable. This is shown in Figure A.2.

Validation

Organizations will still need validation processes to encompass the entire life cycle from initiation through development, testing and installation to support. These processes will generate the documentary evidence to demonstrate that the product or system was developed, tested, implemented and maintained in a controlled manner. In this case the deliverable is the business continuity plan.

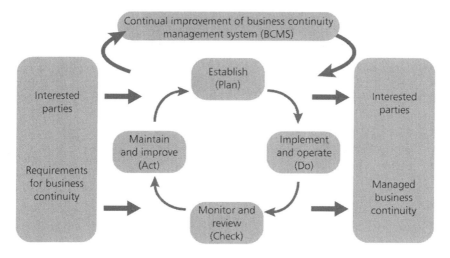

Figure A.2 The PDCA cycle for business continuity

Plan

The business continuity planning project team will go out to business units, customers, trading partners and others to identify the functions and systems that are necessary to keep the organization and its businesses in operation.

After initial analysis of this data has been completed, the key information is documented and verified with the managers and users within the organization to ensure that the situation and its context are understood as fully as possible. Any discrepancies or misunderstandings are fed back into the analysis, and new conclusions presented again. This process will continue until the project team are satisfied that the information held is correct.

At this point the risks facing the organization can be considered in terms of the macro risks facing the entire organization and its business services, as well as the micro risks that face particular systems and processes.

Out of this planning stage comes the specification for, and detailed requirements of, the business continuity plan.

Chapters 2–4 deal with this aspect of the life cycle.

Do

Once the strategy and requirements have been identified it is possible to start building the detail into the plan.

At this stage the documents prepared in the planning stage become important, in particular the business impact analysis. These should be available for all systems and processes and should be regularly updated as processes, risks, environment and other relevant factors change.

A variety of options may be considered. These are then evaluated according to their likely ability to meet the project requirements. The project requirements include the brief prepared by top management and so will reflect the needs of the organization.

One of the options to be addressed is how much risk the organization will accept before it implements the plan and how the plan is to be invoked and used. Additionally there needs to be consideration over whether the plan will rest fully on in-house resources or whether all or any parts of it will be handled by external contractors or outsourcers.

The outcome of the build stage is the business continuity plan.

Chapter 5 deals with this aspect of the life cycle.

Check

Once the plan is in place it is ready to use.

The real problem here is that the plan is only there in case of an incident. There is normally no desire to have an incident just to see if the plan works.

The plan is therefore usually implemented in a controlled way, by testing its assumptions and workings.

The tests usually fall into one of the following categories.

- **Paper-based** (or desk-based) – the principles and actions in the plan are tried out by running through them on paper. This gives an overview of the issues and sequences, but does not test the underlying assumptions or ideas.

- **Limited test** – the principles and actions are tried out in a controlled environment. Certain assumptions will be made but no actual facilities or business units will be closed down to simulate a real incident.
- **Full test** – the principles and actions will be tried out in a real environment. Although facilities and/or business units may be shut down for the test there are likely to be some assumptions made but there will be relatively few of these.

The level of testing will depend upon the organization and its perception of the risks eventuating. The cost and disruption of a full test may deter most organizations from selecting this option, but it is the nearest test to reality that can be made of the recovery plan.

The outcome of the implementation stage is the business continuity plan and ideas and feedback on how it works (or might work) in practice.

Chapters 6 and 7 deal with this aspect of the life cycle.

Act

Once the plan has been published it should not be set in stone.

Feedback will have been received from any tests that have been carried out as well as from those outside the project team who have read the plan and have views on it.

Additionally, the business, its systems, partners and customers will change and evolve over time. These changes need to be appreciated and captured to ensure that the plan is updated to reflect them. The business impact analysis is one of the routes for capturing system and risk changes and there needs to be a process to continue generating and reviewing these from across the organization.

In practice, monitoring means keeping a watching brief over the plan and its supporting processes and dealing with any changes or other issues that may affect it. It is a task that never finishes, as it will be relevant throughout the plan's lifetime.

Any outcomes of the monitoring stage are feed into the planning stage and thus back into the business continuity plan.

Chapters 8 and 9 deal with this aspect of the life cycle.

Audit programmes

The following provides some challenge ideas for an audit of the business continuity life cycle.

Suggested interviewees:

- project manager;
- project sponsor;
- selection of business units that had contributed to the planning data.

Audit objective – plan phase

The aim of this audit work is to ensure that the planning phase leading up to the production of the plan is robust and that it accords with management's intentions as well as organizational, statutory and other guidelines.

- Review the brief from top management on the project parameters.
- Understand the responsibilities of those on the project as well as those advising the project.
- Determine whether the project team obtained sufficient information to enable decisions to be made.
- Determine how the project moved from one phase to another and whether sign offs were required and given.
- Determine whether the organization's procedures and policies were being followed.

Audit objective – do phase

The aim of this audit work is to ensure that the plan has been developed properly using a sound approach and has captured all the relevant information for the organization in the light of its business model and trading links.

- Review and evaluate the procedures for gathering data and information.
- Determine whether the project captured all relevant and available data and information.
- Take a view on whether the conclusions drawn or assumptions made were reasonable given the information and knowledge at the time.
- Consider whether the risks identified were reasonable.

- Determine whether a risk matrix was built up to record all relevant risks envisaged and assess their likely impact.
- Review and evaluate the methodology used to build and populate the plan.
- Where information has been obtained from other functions or partners, look for written evidence that they have agreed the information and/or conclusions drawn from it.
- Determine whether audit trails exist to show the path from information to decision.
- Review samples of questionnaires and other documents to determine if they are designed to facilitate accurate gathering of information.

Audit objective – check phase

The aim of this audit work is to ensure that the plan will work in practice, given that the chaos of a real incident can never be fully captured.

- Review and evaluate the parameters for testing.
- Review documented assumptions, testing procedures and any test data used.
- Review the risk impacts assessed during the tests.
- Review the adequacy of testing performed.
- Determine whether any criteria were set for the tests and, if so, whether they have been met.
- Review documentation generated from the test to ensure it can be used for feedback purposes.
- Review any audit trails linking the plan, through the test, to the feedback documentation.
- Determine whether the organization's testing procedures (if any) were followed.

Audit objective – act phase

The aim of this audit work is to ensure that feedback from the implementation phase and any changes to the organizational systems, business models and trading links are captured and used to improve future iterations of the plan.

- Review and evaluate the processes for undertaking and performing post-implementation monitoring of the plan.

- Review and evaluate the processes for incorporating changes to the basic assumptions and details recorded in the plan.
- Understand how such amendments are captured and recorded in the revised plan.
- Review the feedback documents for completeness and ease of use.

Audit objective – documentation

The aim of this audit work is to ensure that the documentation is complete and accurate and supports the decisions made.

- Obtain and review any documentation standards that may exist to determine whether the business continuity documentation has been prepared correctly.
- Ensure that documentation created conforms to the organization's requirements in terms of security and data classification.
- Ensure that the update process conforms to organizational standards.
- Ensure that the key documentation, such as the plan, is covered by a version control process.
- Check that historical copies of the plan and other key documentation are being retained.
- Ensure that documentation is available to those that are authorized to see it, when they need it.

Appendix 4

Auditing the project

The project

Projects are separate from the day-to-day, 'business as usual' activity in an organization. They are established to control and manage an important change or introduce new processes or systems to the organization. Normally they have a defined start and end, as well as a list of deliverables or goals to achieve or meet.

Setting up a project to develop a business continuity management system and the resultant plan is an ideal way to progress. It allows a dedicated team to explore the concepts and issues, gather data and information from within and outside the organization and develop the solutions and processes appropriate for the organization.

All projects have a number of key stages:

- project outline;
- feasibility study;
- build;
- test;
- implement.

Project outline

The project outline is the document prepared or authorized by top management that sets out a brief statement of the purpose and objectives of the project, including:

- the nature of the project;
- benefits expected;
- anticipated timescale;

- known constraints;
- resources available to the project, including budget.

The project then requires a project manager, who will be responsible for running the project, and ideally a 'project champion', who will be a senior person in the business responsible for supporting the project manager during the project and taking responsibility for the project when it is complete.

For a business continuity project the appointed project manager needs to be able to dedicate sufficient time to drive the project along and to deal with the problems and decisions that will arise.

Feasibility study

This is the most important stage of the project, as it determines how the project will be run. Changes made to the approaches at this stage are cheap; changes made later are progressively more expensive.

This stage turns the bare brief into a series of ideas, tasks and actions. The project team will develop documentation and procedures for data, information and knowledge collection. In turn they will develop methods of analysing and filtering the data to provide succinct but accurate reports on the various issues and requirements found. They will also explore other options for achieving the end result of the plan. These are likely to include co-sourcing and outsourcing, as well as software and other processes that may make the task easier, quicker and more accurate.

To prove the concepts, some of the different options may be explored alongside one another until the best method of working is determined.

The team are also likely to introduce the project to others and explain what is being undertaken and how other business units need to be involved. Similarly, they should talk to outside partners and others who may need to contribute, so appropriate time should be set aside for these discussions.

The project manager should also consider whether a standard project methodology should be used. The organization may already have a preferred approach, in which case the project manager will use that, but if not then the option is available to use another methodology.

The benefits of using a project management methodology are that it:

- separates the management and technical aspects of organization, planning and control;
- facilitates control at all levels;
- makes the project's progress more visible to management;
- provides a communication medium for all project staff;
- ensures that work progresses in the correct sequence;
- involves senior management and users in the project at the right time and place;
- allows the project to be stopped and restarted, completely under management control, at any time in the project's life.

Any methodology or approach used should also allow for the set-up of milestones or decision points. Milestones are significant points in the project, where, say, a key decision must be made or a major deliverable produced. Milestones will have dates assigned to them, and someone will be made accountable for meeting them. Decision points are similar, but mark when decisions must be taken in order to progress the project.

A cost and benefit analysis may also be required as part of this stage if the project team is looking to choose between several options. This may be the case, for example, if outsourcing of the recovery options is being considered.

The final stage of the feasibility study is the decision whether or not to go ahead. In the case of a business continuity project, stopping the process is seldom an option.

Build

Once the data capture and documentation decisions have been made the next stage is to interview the business unit managers and their staff to build a picture of how the organization works. Trading partners, key customers and other players may also have to be visited to complete this picture.

Essentially the idea is to capture data about the existing systems, the way they are interlinked, their contribution to the business and their priority to the business and its objectives.

Against this will need to be built a set of risks that can be applied to these systems and dependencies to understand what would happen if these risks eventuated. Some of the risks will be generic and developed by the project team and others contributing to the project. Others will be specific to the systems or processes being reviewed. A further category of risk is those that have yet to be defined. These are the 'what-if' risks that extend the value of the plan towards catering for a whole range of variables.

Once the plan is built it needs to be reviewed for accuracy and this will involve independent checking as well as feedback from those who were consulted.

Test

Once the plan and supporting documentation is completed, it should be tested to ensure that it is likely to work. Testing should be carried out by the project team in the first instance and is likely to be paper-based (or desk-based) to provide a walk-through of the decisions and actions that need to be taken.

Implement

Once the plan has been proven to work in theory it can be finalized and signed off. This would normally be undertaken by top management, as they commissioned it.

The plan can now be circulated as appropriate, followed by staff and managers being trained in how it should be implemented and used.

Audit view

Any project needs to be appropriately managed. Internal audit should be looking to ensure that this is the case. Audits should therefore be conducted during the project life.

The following are some of the questions that could be asked to ensure that all the management aspects have been considered.

- Is there a project manager with sufficient time and skills?
- Is there a project champion with sufficient commitment and authority?
- Is the organization committed to the project?
- Are the project timescales reasonable?
- Will the goalposts be in the same place at project completion?
- Is there a process in place to handle requirement changes?

- Are business units expecting to support this project?
- Are trading partners and others expecting to contribute to this project?
- Do any key people feel strongly threatened by the project?
- Does the organization have a track record of successful projects?
- Is there a project board or steering group chaired by a senior manager?

The following are some of the questions that could be asked to probe the project itself.

- Does the team have a clear and shared view of the project objectives?
- Is the team focused on the business benefits and opportunities?
- Is the project being carried out in manageable stages?
- Is a pilot project planned?
- Does the team have the necessary interpersonal and technical skills to implement the project?
- Has the team consulted with any experienced advisors?
- Have all the business functions and appropriate external partners been involved in the project?
- Has adequate user training been arranged?
- Has the input of initial data been planned?
- Are the acceptance criteria clear?
- Has testing been carried out?
- Have budgets been prepared for externally produced aspects of the project?
- Is someone responsible for monitoring these externally produced aspects against the budget?

Appendix 5

Document management

There are a number of stages in the management of documents.

Creation

This involves the processes controlling creation of and access to information.

This may include who has the appropriate access or authority level to create the documents, and whether they can be created in any location or only (for example) within organizational premises.

Classification

This involves the processes surrounding the establishment of ownership, accountability and evaluation of the information's content to ensure that documents are adequately controlled and protected throughout their life.

Business continuity documentation may give away a lot of detail about the organization, such as its tolerance to certain types of incident and the names and contact details of key players. It is therefore essential that documents are given a classification that is commensurate with their sensitivity. Once documents are classified they should be handled and used only within the terms of that classification.

A policy document may need to be in place to identify the principles for handling such documents, if one does not already exist. For example, which classifications can be sent by post and which have to go by courier? Storage needs will also differ for the different classifications, as will destruction methods.

Transmission

This involves the processes surrounding controlled movement of information to, through and out of, the organization.

As indicated above, this may be affected by the classification and sensitivity of the documents involved.

Retention

This involves the processes that surround the safe storage of information and the periods for which such information may need to be retained.

In determining the retention periods for different types of information, organizations will need to be aware of any local laws or of any guidance particular to their industry sector. Multinational organizations will also need to be aware that they are operating across multiple jurisdictions and the needs of the different governments may mean that they have to retain information in some jurisdictions longer than actually required in order to meet the needs in another country they operate in.

In the main, these minimum retention periods typically relate to financial information. Business continuity records may, however, also be important in the long term and organizations should develop specific retention policies for them.

Review

This involves the processes surrounding the management of documents.

Once documents are created they take on a life of their own and need to be managed. In many cases this is a simple process in that they are created and used for specific purposes. They are then retained until no longer needed and destroyed.

Business continuity documents are among those on which people will depend. It is therefore vital that users know that they can trust the documents that they are provided with. For this reason there needs to be a complete set of processes in place to ensure this. These processes will include change management and version control. These are discussed more fully in Chapter 8, but primarily ensure that users are only provided with the latest copies and that these can be distinguished from earlier versions to avoid confusion.

Destruction

This involves the processes that surround the effective disposal of information.

Destruction processes need to recognize the sensitivity of the document as well as the medium it is on. For example, paper documents may require shredding, while electronic records may need exposure to magnetic currents or complete physical destruction to ensure they are no longer readable.

Disposal plans should never include throwing such information into an ordinary waste bin. It is too easy for such discarded information to get into the wrong hands and be used to the detriment of the organization.

Appendix 6

Gold-silver-bronze command structure

Command structure

A gold-silver-bronze command structure is used by emergency services of the United Kingdom to establish a hierarchical framework for the effective command and control of major incidents and disasters. By its nature, it also provides a methodology that can be successfully used to undertake a business continuity recovery by any organization.

Although the term 'gold-silver-bronze' is used in business continuity recovery to denote this kind of approach, it is also known as 'strategic, tactical, operational'. As Table A.6 shows, the terms are interchangeable.

Table A.6 Mapping the terminology

Gold	Strategic
Silver	Tactical
Bronze	Operational

Gold/Strategic

The Gold Commander is in overall control of their organization's resources at the incident. They will not be on site, but in a distant control room, usually known as Gold Command. Here they will formulate the strategy for dealing with the incident.

If there are multiple incidents or a Gold Commander for each of the emergency services, they may be co-located. If not, they will be in constant touch with each other.

To a large extent, top management has already undertaken the strategic aspect of a recovery by having a plan developed and delegating responsibility to others to manage the plan. It is therefore not always necessary to have a Gold Commander. However, the overriding control document for the business continuity plan is the incident management plan.

The incident management plan defines how the strategic issues of an incident should be managed. Senior management can then use this to control any incident that is fully, or partially, outside the defined scope of the business continuity plan.

Using senior management to manage an incident is most likely going to take place when the impact is over a wider area than the continuity plan covers. This would include national emergencies, terrorism and pandemics, for example. It may also cover situations not foreseen in the continuity plan, such as hostile takeovers.

Silver/Tactical

The Silver Commander is the senior member of the emergency services at the scene, in charge of all their resources. They decide how to utilize these resources to achieve the strategic aims of the Gold Commander and determine the tactics to be used. At the scene of the incident, they will work in proximity and harmony with other emergency services' Silver Commanders, usually situated in their purpose-built command vehicles. The Silver Commander will not, however, become directly involved in dealing with the incident itself.

This is the normal recovery level for an organization's recovery team, who will be guided by the business continuity plan, as this addresses the tactical aspects of a business incident from the initial response to the point at which normal operations are resumed.

Apart from the responsibilities of the recovery team, the plan should also have detailed the principles for dealing with external players, such as emergency and recovery services.

If the incident is, or moves, outside the scope of the assumptions on which the business continuity plan was based, then the matter should be escalated to those responsible for implementing the incident management plan.

Bronze/Operational

A Bronze Commander directly controls the emergency services' resources at the incident and will be found with their staff working at the scene. If an incident is widespread geographically, different Bronze Commanders may assume responsibility for different areas. If complex, different Bronze Commanders can command different tasks or responsibilities at an incident.

Recovery arrangements at this level will depend on the incident. If it is something involving the emergency services then others may be prevented from accessing the site. If, however, it is an internal incident then organizational staff who are part of the recovery team will be involved. Their responsibilities may range from assessing damage to clearing up and bringing business functions back. Where IT systems are involved then, clearly, IT staff will be used as they would have the necessary skills. The business continuity plan will be used to guide the different processes and who should be involved.

Appendix 7

Business continuity policy statement

Policy statement

Policy statements are important expressions of an organization's culture and environment in the way that they define what staff and contractors are expected to do and the penalties for non-compliance. The method of building policies will vary depending on the organizational culture, but the following paragraphs are based on the approach recommended by ISO/IEC 27002:2005.

Whatever methodology is chosen for building the policy, the final document should be consistent with the layout, format and style of other policies issued by the organization and should have an owner who is responsible for its review and update as discussed later in this section.

Policies and guidelines

To establish the appropriate culture within an organization that will lead to a sound and sustainable business continuity management system, it is necessary for the senior management of the organization to:

- endorse the need for good business continuity practices and promote the concepts;
- establish an appropriate policy to provide the framework for control;
- conform to the published policy, as well as any procedures and guidelines.

Without a written policy in place relating to the continuity of the business in the event of incidents or disasters, the organization will be seen to be showing key weaknesses:

- management does not appear to take the subject seriously;
- there is no responsibility for the ownership of continuity issues;
- there is no accountability for actions;
- there are no safeguards for staff and others;
- no standards can be implemented;
- it may be difficult to impose disciplinary processes for actions undertaken against the organization's interests.

The policy statement

In developing any policy for the organization, it has to be considered whether the organization would be best served by one fully inclusive detailed policy document, or by a high-level policy supported by a range of more detailed policies, standards and guidelines at a lower level. A fully comprehensive policy has advantages, but once it exceeds a page or two, then users are less likely to read it or to remember what they have read. There is therefore an advantage in an organization providing smaller and more compact policies that are easier to read and – due to their job requirements – may not need to be read by all staff.

One other issue that is particularly relevant is the structure of the policy. Most policies contain a series of statements about the things that staff may not do. However, such a list of 'banned' activities quickly becomes out of date as threats change and new ones take their place. There is therefore some shift towards having policies that do not emphasize what *should not be* done, but rather emphasize what *should be* done. Adding the phrase 'business-related' to any activity tends to quickly narrow down whether that action is in support of the organization or not.

Terms of employment

Policies, whatever their nature, should also be related back to the contract of employment, whether for staff or contractors. They should also include a reference to the standard disciplinary processes that the organization has in place.

Disciplinary processes may need to take into account contractors and temporary employees.

As long as staff and contractors are made aware of the do's and don'ts, there should be no problems in pursuing action in the event that things go wrong.

Policy dissemination

Originally all policies were issued in paper format and either given to all staff or placed in prominent locations, such as on noticeboards. Increasingly the paper copy has given way to the electronic version with a consequent movement of the responsibility from management putting the policy in a prominent location to staff having to take time to read and understand the policy when it is issued.

Essentially, the policy should be communicated throughout the organization to users in a form that is relevant, accessible and understandable to the intended reader.

If a policy is sent by electronic mail to all staff or posted on the intranet where any authorized user could access it, this does not signify that users have read or understood it. Ideally, therefore, whenever a policy is issued in this way, staff should be required to signal that they have read, understood and will abide by that policy. For significant policies, such as that covering business continuity, it is often recommended that this certification is not just required when the policy is released, but annually thereafter, to help reinforce its messages.

The form of certification could be in one of a number of ways, but typically may be by:

- signing and returning a tear-off slip on the policy;
- completing an online process to confirm that the policy has been read and understood;
- a copy of the policy being circulated within a section or small department and users signing it;
- a manager confirming that he or she has circulated it to his or her staff and that they have read and understood it.

Induction training may be appropriate for new starters, but there should be initial and ongoing training for all staff, ideally at regular intervals. Temporary and contract staff need special consideration, as their employment may be too short to warrant full training. At the very least, the business continuity policy must dictate what they may and may not do and should be signed by them and form part of their contract of employment with the organization.

Policies, procedures and processes

Underneath the policy may be further documents defining different aspects of the issues involved. These are likely to be key documents that describe:

- individual responsibilities for tasks;
- timescales for completion of events or achievement of milestones;
- detailed procedures for achieving a specific outcome (e.g. resetting an alarm system).

There may be many of these covering a raft of continuity issues but, in the main, they will only apply to small numbers of staff and do not therefore need to be in the policy document. Additionally, as they may be subject to regular change or improvement (for example as staff change jobs) they can be reissued quickly without the need to go through a full policy reissue process.

What should the policy look like?

The overall policy document should be approved by management, and published and communicated, as appropriate, to all employees. It should state the management's commitment and set out the organization's approach to managing business continuity.

As a minimum, the following guidance should be included:

- a definition of business continuity, its overall objectives and scope and its importance;
- a statement of management intent, supporting the goals and principles of business continuity;
- a brief explanation of the policy and the principles required, including:
  - identifying how an incident should be reported;
  - explaining who is responsible for dealing with incidents;
  - the role of staff and contractors in the event of an incident;
  - safety of personnel and ensuring minimum concern to their families;
  - who can speak to the press and other media on behalf of the organization;
  - recovery of the organization.

References to documentation that may support the policy, for example more detailed policies and/or specific procedures for certain categories of staff or activity, may also need to be included depending on their sensitivity.

A sample policy layout is included as Figure A.3 at the end of this appendix.

Policy review and evaluation

The policy should have an owner who is responsible for its maintenance and review according to a defined review process. This process should ensure that a review takes place in response to any changes affecting the basis of the original risk assessment, for example significant incidents, new vulnerabilities or changes to the organization.

There should also be scheduled, periodic reviews of the following:

- the policy's effectiveness, demonstrated by the nature, number and impact of recorded incidents and responses;
- cost and impact of controls on business efficiency;
- effects of changes to the trading environment and technology.

The nature of the policy is likely to be fairly high level. It is therefore unlikely to be dealing with specific systems within the organization. Nor should it name individuals or provide contact information. In view of this, changes should be relatively infrequent and are more likely to follow significant organizational events, such as a move of premises.

Audit view

The first thing that any audit should look for is whether there is a policy in place at all.

Although the organization may have a business continuity plan in place, it may not have a policy. Many simply have statements that exist on noticeboards, on the intranet or in electronic mails to staff.

The problem with this route is that there is no clear ownership of the process or obligation or responsibility on staff to actually do anything or be involved. This is because of the uncertainty that they will have read or understood such notices. A policy imposes a duty on them whereas a statement or electronic mail simply provides information that they may or may not see.

It follows from this that staff almost certainly could not be disciplined if they fail to take any action that leads to the plan not being implemented in time to manage an incident. Disciplining staff may not be what the organization is about, but ensuring that staff acts in the best interests of the organization certainly is.

Audit needs to regularly review all policies, as they are statements of intent by the management.

Table A.7 is a framework of questions to use in assessing a policy statement.

Table A.7 Policy statement questionnaire

Question	Yes	No	Prompts
Is there a business continuity policy in place?			The basic opening question.
Is the policy appropriate for the organization?			Has the policy been crafted for the organization or is it generic or a copy? Does it reflect the size, nature and risk appetite of the organization?
Does it properly reflect any statutory, regulatory, guidance or health and safety responsibilities?			Does it refer back to such guiding authorities to put the seriousness of the issues into context?
Does it give away too much?			Does it provide information that should not be disseminated, such as recovery site telephone numbers or references that would enable a disgruntled employee (or other person) to create problems?
Is it consistent with other policies?			Does it have the same 'look and feel' of other policies, such as the same layout, font, type size?
Is it going to date quickly?			Does it contain information that will rapidly go out of date, such as contact names rather than job titles?

Question	Yes	No	Prompts
Is it up to date?			Does it reflect the situation as it is now?
Does it have an owner?			Is someone within the organization charged with managing, reviewing and updating the policy?
Is this the appropriate owner?			Are all policies owned by the same function (e.g. human resources) and is this the correct owner to ensure that the policy is properly maintained?
Is there a recognized update process and timescale?			Are there documented triggers and procedures for when updates should be considered alongside the general requirement to update when significant events occur?
Has it been disseminated to staff properly?			Is the process to broadcast the policy and its aims robust? Does it work?
Is it available to all staff (including temporary staff) and to contractors?			Did it go to all categories of staff? Do contractors sign it as part of their contract?
Is it understood and followed?			From discussions with staff outside the business continuity area, is it clear that they understand their roles and responsibilities?
Do managers or staff have defined responsibilities and have they been trained for these?			Is the policy actually going to work? If managers and staff cannot fulfil their roles then there is a problem.

Question	Yes	No	Prompts
Is there a disciplinary process?			Are the penalties for breaching the policy clearly laid out? Do these penalties conform to the terms of employment? Are appropriate penalties in place for temporary staff and contractors? Are they aware of these, as they may not be specifically quoted in the policy?
In any tests or live incidents has the policy been invoked?			This is the true test of whether the policy actually works.

NOTE: For completion in the field, the above questionnaire requires the 'prompts' column to be replaced by a blank 'comments' column to capture any observations about the findings. The questionnaires will then also serve as part of the audit working papers.

The questions in the matrix stem from issues that have been found across a number of organizations of different sizes and sectors.

It has also been noted that where a trade body or pressure group has provided a policy for its members or adherents to follow it is often that exact policy wording that is used in multiple organizations. The wording, terminology and concepts may be at odds with other policies provided by the organization. In addition, the values and ideals may be correct but the organization may actually do more or less than the generic example. The policy needs to reflect this, otherwise staff will feel that they are being misrepresented.

Where policies have been imported from other places there may be less of an acceptance or adherence by staff, as they do not feel any 'ownership' of the issues involved. This can be a problem where a generic policy or one drafted by an outsourcer is involved.

The following is the sequence of events from one organization intending to develop a business continuity process.

- *An electronic mail was sent to all staff saying that a business continuity programme was important and was going to be implemented.*

- *Some statements about staff responsibilities appeared on the intranet.*
- *One of these statements said managers would be responsible for instructing their staff in their business continuity role.*
- *IT led the project to bring in the business continuity plan.*
- *IT outsourced the responsibility for development of the plan.*
- *Audit were told they could not review the project until the whole process was completed.*
- *No arrangements were put in place to train managers or staff or make them aware of their responsibilities.*
- *The process is not touching staff and they have no buy-in to what is happening.*

Perhaps not surprisingly, the project continues to drag on. Agreed, many other issues are highlighted here but with no policy there is no buy-in and no responsibility.

Outsourcers and their policies

An organization that uses outsourced recovery processes or procedures or has working relationships with other organizations that create any form of dependency needs to be sure that its outsourcers and partners will also be able to cope with an incident.

The questions that need to be asked are as follows.

- Do their incidents affect me?
- Does my incident affect them?
- Do we have shared actions that need to be coordinated?

As part of this appreciation, internal audit needs to have access to the outsourcer to check the policy and cross-reference it with the organization's policy to ensure that there are no conflicts.

To facilitate this there will need to be provision in the outsourcing contract to ensure that internal audit can gain access to the outsourcer to conduct this and other checks.

Audit view

Internal audit will need to work with the outsourcers and partners to ensure that the approach to business continuity is common and that the actions of one party will not jeopardize the others. Any assumptions will need to be identified, as these may have a big impact on what actually happens in an incident.

This is a sensitive role and will require audit to challenge the assumptions behind the policies within the various organizations and take a view on the likely outcome of any incident on the relationships and system involved.

The matrix in Table A.7 will work for any policy and will help correlate the findings of the review.

Inconsistencies between policies are to be expected and, as internal audit has no role outside its own organization, such issues can only be flagged rather than acted upon. Nevertheless a close working relationship should mean that such issues are addressed even if it is by way of procedural rather than policy changes.

Policy statement layout

Figure A.3 is included as a possible layout for a business continuity policy developed in accordance with the guidance in ISO/IEC 27002:2005 and its predecessors. It is provided only as an illustration of how such a policy document could be formulated.

The information provided in it conforms to the requirements of ISO 22301, 5.3.

Figure A.3 Sample business continuity policy statement layout

Introduction

This section introduces the purpose of the policy.

It would normally provide a high-level overview explaining that business continuity is essential for safeguarding the business and ensuring that plans are in place to protect the organization and its employees in the event of an incident or disruption.

There is no need for a detailed discussion of the business continuity plan.

Scope of policy

This section explains who the policy applies to and which parts of the organization it affects.

Normally it will apply to all staff and contractors in all locations of the organization.

Objective of the policy

This section summarizes the objective of the policy, which is to keep the business going in the event of an incident.

A simple statement such as: 'To ensure business continuity and minimize business damage by preventing and reducing the impact of incidents' may be sufficient.

Purpose of the policy

This section summarizes the purpose of the policy.

Where the objective is to ensure business continuity, the purpose is actually to protect the organizational assets (which include people) from all threats, whether internal or external, deliberate or accidental.

Statement of policy

This section provides a set of statements that make up the policy. Bullet points are easier for readers to understand and work well in this section.

There will be a number of statements according to organizational needs and they might include:

- staff and contractors must promptly notify management of all conditions that could lead to a disruption of business activities;
- all electronically held corporate data or information must be backed up as directed by the IT function;
- procedures and processes must be in place to ensure that training on business continuity is available and given as required and necessary;
- all business unit managers must ensure that any changes to systems, interdependencies or other factors affecting business continuity are drawn to the attention of the business continuity team.

Compliance

This section records under whose authority the policy has been issued (such as the chief executive officer) and states that compliance with its principles is mandatory for all employees and contractors.

Breaches

This section details what happens in the event that someone breaches any of the statements in the policy. Note that employees and others can only be disciplined for breaching stated policies, so the wording of those policies needs to be reasonably wide to cover a range of eventualities.

Usually it will link back to terms of employment for employees or contracts for others, which will detail the penalties for breach of any disciplinary code. The opportunity may also be taken to explain that although there is an internal disciplinary process, the organization does not preclude pursuing any action through the courts.

Definition

This section provides any required legal definitions of the organization, its subsidiaries, affiliates, and so on that may affect the legal standing of the policy.

Interpretation

This section details which business unit is responsible for the policy and who will provide interpretations or manage issues that may arise from the implementation and use of the policy. This unit would normally also be responsible for policy reviews and updates.

Undertaking

This section provides for the employee or contractor to sign to indicate that they have read, understood and accept the business continuity policy.

NAME _____

SIGNED _____

DATE _____

Further reading

Websites

Websites referenced were available in May 2012.

In many cases it is necessary to search the sites using the phrase 'business continuity' to find the relevant pages.

The British Standards Institution
http://www.bsigroup.com

International Organization for Standardization
http://www.iso.org

The Business Continuity Institute
The Good Practice Guides
http://www.thebci.org/

Chartered Management Institute
Annual business continuity management survey
http://www.managers.org.uk

Financial Services Authority (FSA)
Business continuity management practice guide, also material on pandemics
http://www.fsa.gov.uk

International Accreditation Forum
World association of conformity assessment accreditation bodies
http://www.iaf.nu/

Business Continuity and Disaster Recovery Education and Certification Institute
Singapore, Malaysia and Thailand
http://www.bcm-institute.org

The Chartered Institute of Internal Auditors
http://www.iia.org.uk

The Institute of Internal Auditors
http://www.theiia.org

Infosecurity Europe
Annual information security breaches survey
http://www.infosec.co.uk

Publications

BS 25999-1:2006, *Business continuity management — Part 1: Code of practice*

BS 25999-2:2007, *Business continuity management — Part 2: Specification*

ISO/IEC 22301:2012, *Societal security — Business continuity management systems — Requirements*

ISO/TR 22312:2011, *Societal Security — Technological Capabilities*

ISO 22320:2011, *Societal security — Emergency management — Requirements for incident response*

ISO/PAS 22399:2007, *Societal security — Guideline for incident preparedness and operational continuity management*

ISO/IEC 24762:2008, *Information technology — Security techniques — Guidelines for information and communications technology disaster recovery services*

ISO/IEC 27001:2005, *Information technology — Security techniques —Information security management systems — Requirements*

ISO/IEC 27002:2005, *Information technology — Security techniques — Code of practice for information security management*

ISO/IEC 27031:2011, *Information technology — Security techniques — Guidelines for information and communication technology readiness for business continuity*

ISO 31000:2009, *Risk management — Principles and guidelines*

ASIS/BSI BCM.01:2010, *Business continuity management systems: Requirements with guidance for use*

AS/NZS 5050:2010, *Business continuity — Managing disruption related risk*

SI 24001:2007, *Security and continuity management systems — Requirements and guidance for use*

SS 540:2008, *Business continuity management (BCM)*

IIA – UK and Ireland (2001) *IT Disaster Recovery, A Guide for Internal Auditors – Information Technology Briefing Note*, London: IIA – UK and Ireland

Marcella, AJ, Stucki, C (2004) *Business Continuity, Disaster Recovery and Incident Management Planning: A Resource for Ensuring Ongoing Enterprise Operations*, Maitland, FL: The Institute of Internal Auditors Research Foundation